Twilight
of the
Gods

My adventures with The Who

Tony Klinger

JOHN BLAKE

Published by John Blake Publishing Ltd,
3 Bramber Court, 2 Bramber Road,
London W14 9PB, England

www.johnblakepublishing.co.uk

First published in hardback in 2009

ISBN: 978-1-84454-766-1

British Library Cataloguing-in-Publication Data:

A catalogue record for this book is available from the British Library.

Design by www.envydesign.co.uk

Printed in the UK by CPI William Clowes Beccles NR34 7TL

1 3 5 7 9 10 8 6 4 2

Papers used by John Blake Publishing are natural, recyclable products made from
wood grown in sustainable forests. The manufacturing processes conform to the
environmental regulations of the country of origin.

Plate section p1 author's collection, p2-8 © Rex Features

I dedicate this book to all the fools, like me, who have the entertainment industry flowing through their bloodstream.

Foreword

Why this book? It is my account of a time and a place, of making films and a group called The Who. Together, like it or not, we made a special documentary feature-length movie called *The Kids Are Alright*, named after one of their songs, which have the happy habit of turning into anthems for their place and time. Almost all the main players in this drama about the film's production were in their twenties or thirties when this story was taking place in the early 1970s. I was a young but relatively experienced filmmaker of about 26 when it started, and about 28 when it ended, although I felt like an old geezer.

It is also an attempt to put the record straight. It's natural for people to remember stories and incidents to suit themselves but I have tried to be accurate and my record-keeping was good. It helps that my memories were written at the same time as or soon after the events concerned, and I was always straight when I worked — I never used heavy drugs, which cloud and distort memory. But I was always too busy to deal with the past when the future was beckoning. I have always wanted to get on with the present and take the future as it comes. I had simply walked away. Now I'm older I have returned. It's time that someone recounted these events with some accuracy.

During the filming of the first sequences at Shepperton Film Studios, I knew we were capturing lightning in a bottle. Watching The Who strut their stuff in the studio was so exciting I couldn't believe what was happening and neither could anyone else. It had been a very long time since they'd played together and there were fears that they would never do so again. None of us had had any real idea if they would even turn up, let alone be able to play together with such passion, energy or fun. But it was always a struggle to make it through to the finishing line of this film.

I should set the scene here. There were two camps in the band, and there was virtually no chance of getting them all together to talk about what we hoped to do with them. Instead, it was a series of phone calls to individuals, then getting back to the first bloke and telling them the second bloke had said OK, followed by begging calls to their manager, Bill Curbishley, who would say yes or no to the final plan. It was tortuous and long-winded, and compounded by the fact that there were also two camps in the film team. It was a nightmare to organise anything in this environment and the only really good times were when we actually got to film something and no one was plotting and planning in an office.

I also understood that we were doing something that

couldn't happen again. I realised immediately after our first meeting that it would be a miracle if Keith Moon lived long enough to attend the film's premiere, and that a way of life for our generation was changing. We were becoming more self-aware, less self-indulgent and even a bit more health-conscious. These were strange times indeed.

I don't pretend to have great musical knowledge, but I do know what sets British rock'n'roll apart from the rest. It is the music of our streets; it's the sound of our angry, confused and sometimes incoherent young. It's considered middle class but straddles a much wider demographic. As soul and R&B symbolise the black working-class experience of America, so working-class, angry rock is the English sound. That anger in the singing and playing is the difference between pop and rock; it's not just about a nice tune you can hum. There's a genuineness to rock that transcends the moment and has a proper place in our society.

The thing you have to remember about all the players here, and in particular the band, is that they are very English. In this global age, that might seem an unimportant part of the mix, but you'd be wrong. Our Englishness sums us all up (Jeff Stein excepted), and explains many of the things about us all and our chippy little attitudes, and innate toughness and aggression. The English do like a bit of a fight. Under the veneer of sophistication and a long history of manners is the real England, built by pirates and driven by a genius for creativity and the construction of great things – and their destruction. The Who sum this up.

No one writes songs like Townshend. He really is a

unique talent whose music has stood the test of time and his compositions sound as current now as the day they first smashed into our consciousness in the 1960s. There were other artists with as much or more talent at one aspect of what The Who did, but no one passed them for a talent for achievement and living. They were the unedited version of what a rock'n'roll band is supposed to be, with bells on.

People always want to hear Who 'war' stories and the reason is obvious. As a group The Who were more fun, explosive and interesting than almost all the rest. One of my particular favourites was told to me by Dougal Butler, the man who managed Keith Moon's personal affairs. This is an easy job with a normal person, but minding Keith Moon was like looking after a nursery full of small kids and a zoo of wild goats, while herding some cats.

The story goes that Dougal, a natural gentlemen, and Keith were guests in a pleasant little English boutique hotel. The owner had somewhat foolishly reminded Keith that he hadn't actually done anything outlandish in the two or three days he'd been there. This was too much of a challenge for Moon to resist, and he directed Dougal to remodel the establishment using their car. Bish, bosh, bash went the car, into some hedges and through the French windows until it came to a halt inside the building. Too late the owner realised he had unleashed the genie from the bottle, but his protests simply encouraged Keith to new excesses. Dougal and Keith continued their destruction, backing the car into the cupboards, wardrobes and everything else in the room until there wasn't much left in one piece.

The owner was shocked beyond coherence, but Keith somehow contrived to involve him in this mad trail of rampant destruction. Before he knew it, the owner had joined Keith and Dougal in smashing the place to small pieces. That's how it was with Keith. He could suck you into his mayhem like the big kid he was, and before you knew it you too were behaving like a twat.

Most of the stuff around a rock band seems harmless enough to the people listening to the stories of excessive drink, drugs and wild behaviour. But I had always been aware of the darker side. Some of the people around rock music in the last decades of the 20th century were hard men and some were crazy men; it was when the two combined you really had to be careful. Men like Led Zeppelin's manager Pete Grant or Don Arden, who managed ELO, were not nice men to be around. They could be pleasant, even great company, but you didn't want to upset or cross them. Arden in particular liked to tell you stories from his notorious past, loudly and never without a laugh. These were characters who could make you chuckle, as long as you weren't in business with them.

I am a great believer in fate. I had not thought about The Who or this time in my life for many years as I waited for two of my Californian grandchildren, Maya and Sol, after their swimming class one pleasant, sunny day. As I sat there, I heard a radio from the car park and drifted closer as I heard a familiar tune. It was 'Who Are You?' and I remembered the first time I'd played Pete Townshend's demo of it in my car thirty-odd years earlier. I enjoyed it, just as I always had, and then on came Pete, who was being interviewed about his career. He sounded avuncular, amusing and totally normal – much more relaxed and pleasant than I remembered him. He was plainly enjoying recounting stories of his life and it occurred to me that I should do the same.

Many biographies of international rock stars have been written, most of them by people of one or two categories – fans or knockers – who never knew their subjects personally. This book is about three years in the life of a rock band by someone making a film with them, someone who was there. It will be called an exposé by some because it unearths and brings to the public's attention the truth behind the façade. Some might term it revenge, but it's never that. As the Chinese philosopher Confucius said, if you are going to seek revenge, first dig two graves. Others might say I'm just an opportunist seeking to make easy money, but if that were the case I'd have done it 30 years ago, when I could have made a great deal more money from it.

In fact, I did receive earlier offers to tell my story, but not enough water had flowed under the bridge by then and I had other fish to fry. Now I am much older, time has healed the wounds and I have left it long enough for my reflections to be sober and measured. Eventually, the anger cools and, if you're still standing, you can begin to appreciate yourself and others much better. Now I'm ready to let it go. Besides, I want to see the surprise on my children's faces when they read this story and realise their old man wasn't always the old geezer dozing by the telly.

This book isn't meant to be a documentary. This story is a saga of dreams that crashed in on themselves, and this book is my way of exorcising the nightmare it became. What it does is give the reader a vibrant, vividly coloured impression rather than a bland snapshot, but I can promise that I've done everything to be scrupulously fair and honest throughout. I have not set out to hurt anyone, and when in doubt I have left it out.

I always hated that expression Oliver Stone used when defending one of his films – *JFK* I think. When asked if it was the truth (as he had toyed with some historical facts), he said something like, 'It's my truth.' It sounds such a fake statement when someone else says this, but it is accurate. I'm sure, over three decades, that some of the incidents I remember one way will be remembered by someone else another way, but it is my truth.

This book is about the making, breaking and waking up of Tony Klinger around The Who. You either bend at the knee around The Who or you have to fight. This story really did happen and, in telling the tale, I'll upset and anger people but I've kept good records and some things you can't forget even when you want to. I don't know if any of the people who made this film were ever whole again afterwards. It was worse for others than it was for me. Sydney Rose, the executive producer who died recently, suffered health problems from the time production commenced.

I guess in making this film The Who wanted to set their own place in history but required hired guns like me to achieve this. Their hope was to immortalise their place in rock history. My hope was to have fun, get a good credit and make some money. Logically, *The Kids Are Alright* should never have happened. All of us knew enough to see the problems that were sure to come if we made this film, but equally all of us lived at least part of our life behind rose-coloured glasses.

But, before you can understand the making of the film, you need to understand the context of the band in the world. So, without further ado...

1

The End Before The Beginning

What I remember: massive egos, girls, shouting, threats, lawyers coming at you, anonymous death threats, managers screaming, friends, confusion — but, above all, the music.

It's early afternoon at Shepperton Film Studios in the late 1970s. The Who are about to play a small, private gig, to be filmed for a movie that I have agreed to produce. The small invited crowd shouts and cheers as they wait for the band to hit the stage. They are excited — the sweat is pouring off some of them, like overheated animals knowing they're going to get some exercise. The cameras and lights are in position.

I put my head around a corner, thinking that this is where the band is. We have fought our way to this point, but despite the clashes I want to wish them luck. I enter a dressing room but it's the wrong door. I'm hit in the face with the strong smell of heavy joint usage, and instead of the band there are six gnarled, hairy old roadies clad in their uniform of jeans, T-shirts and trainers. They have a girl with them. She looks like a groupie in training: young but not too young (maybe 18 or 19), small, long dark hair, not too pretty but with a great body, one that I can see very well as she is almost totally naked.

The men lift her in the air and pass her from hand to hand like a parcel. They are taking off the last bits of her black underwear, kissing and fondling her as she laughs, lost in a joke and a world all of her own. Everyone is giggling. They are sharing a couple of joints, and groping and squeezing the girl as if they are testing a piece of fruit to see if it's ripe. A couple of them are taking their own clothes off now, and it's turning into an orgy.

One of the guys looks up at my surprised face and says in a Cockney accent, 'Shut the door, mate — it's bloody drafty round the whatsits!' He gently pinches the girl's pert nipple and she laughs as she looks at me through half-closed eyes and blows me a kiss. Another of the men kisses her boobs and strokes her body. She moans in simulated passion and I shut the door.

No one from the band or front-line staff is involved — in fact, I don't recognise any of them. It's one of the less well-known perks of working with a famous band: there are many available and willing women who will make do with the support staff when the famous guys are busy.

I turn down another long corridor and bump into my executive producer, Sydney Rose. 'It would probably be better if you hadn't come, Tony,' he says.

'How's it going?' I ask, ignoring his downbeat greeting.

'You know,' he says, with an expressive shrug.

Yes, I do know — same old nut house.

Keith Moon comes around the corner but virtually ignores us, which is difficult in the narrow corridor. Then he seems to recognise us. 'Hello, chaps,' he says. 'I'm just on my way for some quick brandies — that's what we all need, don't you think!' He marches off down the corridor without us, like a character in *Alice Through the Looking Glass*, larger than life and full of mad surprises.

'Do you know where the boys are so I can wish them luck?' I ask Sydney.

'It isn't a good idea,' he responds. 'The Who don't even know we're going to be here.'

How sad, I reflect, that a film's producer and executive producer should need an invite to be on the set of their own film. Welcome to *The Kids Are Alright*.

Pete Townshend marches past with barely a glance at us. Then he stops, turns towards me and smiles warmly. 'Hello! It's been a long time — how are you?' he asks with great friendship.

'Great,' I answer. 'How's it with you?'

Before we can take it any further, he starts to turn away, but stops again. 'See you later!' he calls over his shoulder as he walks away.

'You see?' I say to Sydney. 'That wasn't so bad, was it?'

It isn't the madness that attracts me, although that can be fun, it's the music. If you like The Who's music then you love it, and if you love it you can't get it out of your head.

If you're not convinced, get hold of a copy of *Live at Leeds* and play it for yourself.

It's that skinny bastard Townshend whirling his long, pipe-stem arms as he plays the guitar – not brilliantly, but with a genuine passion that more than compensates. It's the little blond geezer in the front with the curly hair, snarling out the lyrics with venom, like you should if you want to be a rock'n'roller. Daltrey whips that microphone around his head so fast, it's as if it's a weapon, and maybe it is. Moon is getting pumped full of oxygen just to keep playing, the energy seeping out of his tired and bloated little body, now just a used-up shell. While the lunatic on drums is playing the fills, the beat comes from the bass guitar with metronomic intensity, played by that miserable-looking sod John Entwistle. No one else does it like this, and no one else can.

After the mini-concert, I walk over to Townshend to congratulate him on the band's performance. In the same spirit of friendship, I put out my hand to shake his. He ignores me as if we had never met, turns on his heel and walks away.

As if by some divine signal, the stage lights are extinguished, and each member of the band vanishes into the night with their separate entourages, their own small exclusive and cocooned worlds. All of us are unaware that this was the final gig, the last time all four original members of The Who would ever play together on stage. This was the twilight of the gods.

2

In The Beginning

In the late 1940s, West London was just puffing at the fag end of World War II. It was a shambling wreck of a place, very different to the vibrant, colourful London we know now. It should have been great — after all, we won the bloody war — but the price had been high. Too many men who fought hadn't come home, or the experience of fighting for so many years away from home had changed them — lessened some, made others bigger, but blunted most.

During the war, women had got used to making their own way, earning their own money, making their own fun. Some of them had learned how to say no, and it was from this point that they realised they didn't have to continue with the old ways any more. Their children were going to be different, bound to be.

For years after the war, London was pockmarked with bombsites and unsafe buildings. Everything was grey and a bit dirty with the grime of a lost Empire; dust seemed to encrust our lives. Everything was black and white, even our dreams. There were tramlines in some parts of town, and overhead wires for the trolley buses. Linoleum was on the floor of our houses, and we learned to crawl on its shiny surface. The small fires in the front lounge were surrounded by brown tiles and the fire was made with coal that burned dirty. There was little fruit out of season, and none of it was fancy. The shops usually closed at six sharp and were shut tight on Sundays.

It was flash for any family to have a black-and-white television, and that only really became a possibility with the Queen's coronation in 1953. Radio was still the national entertainment. We got most of our news from the BBC, and our newspapers. The mentality and class structure were still Edwardian. There were hardly any people who weren't white and British. Big girls still wore stockings and pointy bras. Bloody hell, some sweets were still rationed!

Despite the odd unexploded bomb, it was considered safe to play outside with your mates. If there were any child molesters around, we didn't know anything about them. Life for children was a perfect idyll: you played outside until it got dark. We played games of daring, pretending to be cowboys and Indians, and, if you were really lucky, you had one of those Davy Crockett fur hats with a little tail to go with your six-shooter and holster, because no one wanted to be the Indian.

It was into this world that Roger Harry Daltrey arrived on 1 March 1944, in Shepherds Bush, West London. Is it fanciful to wonder if he emerged such an aggressive, sparky little character, or did that come later? Seven months later, on 9 October, John Alec Entwistle followed a couple of miles away in Chiswick, probably scowling but keeping perfect time.

On 19 May 1945, Peter Dennis Blandford Townshend was born, also in Chiswick, just ten days after the Nazi surrender. His father, Cliff, was a professional saxophonist and his mother, Betty, was a singer. Perhaps some of Pete's later stage presence is inherited from his parents.

Finally, on 23 August 1946, Keith John Moon came into this world, in Wembley, Middlesex. Stand well back, everybody. This is the boy who will never grow up. Like a big mucky puppy he is going to be loved by everyone he wags his tail at, but not in their homes. He already has the big chocolate-button eyes, and more mischief travels through his veins than in any ten normal people put together. Drunken nights, endless evenings pretending to be someone he's not, the big orgies, the car in the pool, the water bed in the elevator, the dynamite down the toilet, the televisions thrown from bedrooms, the hotels trashed around the world... Some of these stories will even turn out to be true but they're a long way ahead yet, and the craziness he will unleash on an unsuspecting world masks his never-ending insecurity.

These are normal, naughty English boys; they like to make a lot of noise. It's important to know that they are a product of this very specific place and time, when London was finding a new place for itself in the world after the war. When they finally get together, the noise from these boys will be amplified and become a sound, and it will be called rock music. Many people are going to like that music, and they'll join in, jump around a bit, dance and look cool. They'll buy recordings of that music, and the group who make the noise will be called The Who.

In January 1950, not far away in West Acton, another little boy is born. This smashing child is Tony Klinger. My grandparents tell me they come from far-off places called Russia and Poland, and – I'm told quietly – before that from Germany. In 1950s London, this is not a particularly good thing: the country very clearly hates and resents everything German. But when you're a little kid it's a bit difficult explaining that the Germans have also done a pretty good job wiping out most of that side of my family, because we were considered their enemy too, with our being Jewish.

At the time, most English boys, including me, were hard-wired to comic books portraying British heroism in the face of the evil Nazis. The first foreign language we knew anything about were those bubbles of dialogue from surprised German defenders as British soldiers crashed into them: '*Achtung! Ein Englander!*'

I was also reading comics like *Dandy* and *Beano*, and later science-fiction pilot Dan Dare in *Eagle*. I developed an overwhelming stutter that was only removed a few years later with the blessed help of a gifted teacher, who is now probably teaching English, elocution and speech therapy in heaven. Thank you, Miss Derby, for making that stutter vanish! I also enjoyed a cordial relationship with a large imaginary friend, who had to have his own place every time we ate. I don't think I cared about anything other than having as much fun as possible.

I remember listening via terrible earphones that always fell out, to a tiny, tinny radio with a black leatherette cover under the blankets of the bed in the room I shared with my sister. There was this wonderful station called Radio Luxembourg that played 'pop' tunes from America, and it was wonderful and slightly illicit, even though we had no idea why. While I was listening to these exciting sounds, not far away the boys who were going to be The Who were learning to play their instruments, being just a few years older than me.

We had the top half of what we English called a maisonette, and downstairs lived an ever-changing cast of American military characters who were stationed in not so jolly old austerity England. One of them was a sergeant who worked in something called the PX, which was like an American forces supermarket well before any of us Brits had ever heard of such wonders. He had a ready smile and was the first black person I had ever seen. This was a very positive experience as he provided me with multi-flavoured chewing gum and bubble gum. This was unheard of by my envious friends or me, and this man achieved almost God-like status in my mind. Oh, the sheer joy that man gave me with those different-flavour chewing gums!

When I was about four or five years old, I was made to wear an itchy blue uniform. I quite liked the colour combination with the grey shirt, but didn't understand the reason for the new clothes until I was forced to go to my new, very grown-up primary school, St Francis. It turned out that I was the first non-Catholic to attend the place. In retrospect, I think that my Jewish parents must have been closet anti-Semites. It was very scary to get called out on your first day in the assembly by the headmaster. 'And we all should welcome the new boy, Klinger, who is the first Jewish boy to attend this school, and we shall all make him especially welcome.'

I still remember the heads of the other students swivelling to look me over, their eyes like hundreds of cold gun barrels measuring me as a target.

Shortly afterwards at break-time, a bigger boy called Tony Bartoldi — he seemed a giant and must have been at least nine or ten — approached me in the playground. 'Why did you kill Jesus?' he asked.

Before I could respond that I didn't know any Jesus, let alone kill him, he hit me on the nose, drawing blood and some tears.

When I went home, my family taught me how to box. 'Next time,' my dad said, 'hit them first, and give them something to hate you for.'

This advice coloured much of my later thinking. I became a member of the boxing team at my next school. No one has ever got away cheaply with pushing me around since that day. I try to get my revenge in first.

3

Serendipity

My dad, Michael Klinger, who later produced and put together such films as *Repulsion*, *Cul de Sac* and *Get Carter* — to say nothing of the *Confessions* series and many others — had his first film-business offices in Old Compton Street in London's Soho, where he was born. Dad, who had started to build some club cinemas, was now going into distribution. How odd that just a few doors down were the offices of Track Records, The Who's recording company, before they even knew they were The Who. It meant that we were all in the same orbit, imbibing the same air, and influenced by the same stuff.

Another bit of strange synergy was the fact that I had spent some of my early years growing up in the same part of suburban West London as the members of the band. But, as I later found out, this meant little more than we had similar accents when we insulted each other.

The mid-1960s was a period in which you picked sides

culturally, as a fan and as a person. You had to be a Mod or a Rocker, a flower child or a city type, and the music at the time divided us mainly into those who followed The Beatles or The Stones. Huffing and puffing along in their wake were all the rest, including all the American bands. I must have been a bit of a freak, as I liked all of them. The Motown groups were my favourites for dancing, The Beatles for listening and The Stones for partying.

All of this held true until I saw a little band in London's Soho who turned out to be The Who. They weren't even the best band in the street, but they were the most exciting and different. I fell in love with them, there, live on stage. This was to remain their natural habitat: they have always been fantastic to watch as well as listen to. This never diminished; they never became a caricature of themselves like all the rest. Some of them have died, but they have never relented, never become less, never backed off.

The Who had their genesis at Acton Grammar School, where Roger Daltrey had formed a group called The Detours, including John Entwistle and Pete Townshend on guitars. It was only some time later, after changing their name to The Who then to The High Numbers and back to The Who, that they found a 17-year-old Keith Moon to join them on the drums.

'We were playing a pub in Shepherds Bush,' Roger told me, 'when a geezer dressed head to toe in red, with red hair and pissed out of his brain comes pushing on to the stage and sort of just takes over the drumming job. There was no way we were gonna argue with a nutter like that so we let this audition continue. In fact, I think he thinks he's still bloody well auditioning.'

By 1964, the group had already spent a couple years playing clubs and pubs near their native West London and had made their first record 'I'm the Face', which wasn't a hit. Their next record came after appointing Chris Stamp and Kit Lambert as their co-managers and reverting to the name The Who. This effort was called 'I Can't Explain' and was their first big UK success. More significantly, it established their signature theme capturing English youth's frustrations with the established order of society. Pete Townshend had tapped into the souls of the angry and rebellious young of the 1960s and his songs of the period remain rock classics — 'Anyway, Anyhow, Anywhere', 'Substitute', 'I'm a Boy', 'Happy Jack' and many others.

But, above all, Pete wrote one song that broke them in America and the rest of the world. That song was 'My Generation'. It would have been easy to stay with a repeating flow of similar material, but instead Pete wrote possibly the most innovative and important piece of rock music of the decade, the world's first rock opera, *Tommy*. This went on to become not only widely accepted as a masterwork but it was also the only album to reach the top spot in the US charts on three separate occasions in three different versions — a remarkably vivid artistic and commercial justification of the risk taken in this change of their musical direction.

But nothing in creation comes out of a total vacuum and

the seed for *Tommy* was the witty and biting 'A Quick One', a mini-opera that ran for more than eight minutes in an age when two and a half minutes was the usual length for singles. Pete says it was 'A Quick One' that inspired the idea of *Sgt. Pepper's Lonely Hearts Club Band* – Paul McCartney supposedly admitted as much to him. Thus, one long song seems to have given birth to two of the best and most important rock albums in a generation.

The deceptively simple idea of telling a story to a rock-music background was a revolutionary step from trying to hammer out a message in less than three minutes. In fact, 'A Quick One' came about when Kit Lambert, the group's manager, asked Pete to compose something 'linear' to fill the eight- to ten-minute gap at the end of The Who's second album. Pete said he couldn't imagine any song lasting longer than three minutes, let alone write one, so Lambert told him to write three three-minute songs and join them together. That's how musical history was created!

Because of a mixture of luck and ease with language, communicating my ideas to people is seemingly no problem. I love both modern music and film, and always have done. At this stage, my connection to The Who was purely that of a fan, while my career had been on every rung of the film-production ladder, from tea boy to boss in less than a decade.

My creative streak had kicked in early. While still at school, I won two first prizes from national writing competitions and by the age of 18 I was making small professional films that got public distribution. I began my career in television as an assistant director and then editor, before going on to senior production roles in action-adventure movies such as *Gold* (1974) starring Roger Moore, and *Shout at the Devil* (1976) with Lee Marvin and Moore then to work with Deep Purple on *Rises Over Japan* (for TV) and *The Butterfly Ball* (as co-producer-writer-director). I'd even won an award or two.

What you're meant to do as a producer is gather all the elements of a film together – money, director, artists, distributors, scripts, etc. – and motivate, push, guide and manage them all. The director has to run the picture artistically from the moment he's hired until the film has finished editing.

Loving your work as a film producer and director isn't hard. Someone comes along and gives you money to organise a large bunch of grown-up children (actors), get them into their costumes, make sure they say their lines more or less in order and emote all over the place, and generally make sure everyone is suitably in awe of your genius and incredibly artistic mind. Most of which is bollocks, because it's common knowledge in the movie business that most directors could be replaced by your average traffic cop. Similarly, most producers could be replaced by any used-car salesman. Of course, good producers do run their films well, as do good directors, but they're the exception-which I have always aimed to be.

My experiences as a 'governor' had begun at 18 when I started to write, produce and direct documentaries with my best friend and partner, Mike Lytton. After a few successes, which were a mixture of talent, luck, very hard work and sheer bloodymindedness, we went our separate ways.

By the time I was in my mid-twenties, I had a lot of experience. While making *Shout at the Devil*, Moore had hugely enjoyed my discomfort in a dug-out canoe on an African river after I'd been stung that morning by a scorpion. 'You know you'll die from that, Klinger,' he called out from his boat. 'Scorpion stings are lethal, you know. At the very least, you'll lose the foot.'

At this my mother, who was anxiously visiting the set, called out from the riverbank, 'Don't take any notice, Tutela!' (*Tutela* is a Germanic Yiddish term of endearment from a parent to their child, meaning 'dear little one'.) Once Moore knew this, he was merciless and I became known as Tuts.

We also had the wild and wonderful Lee Marvin starring in the same movie. During it we were filming a battle scene between a World War I German cruiser and a British Vickers Gunbus aircraft we'd built on the River Umzimbubu, and I had placed myself on a bluff to make sure no modern vehicles or people came unwittingly into view of our cameras. Marvin was not required on set that day and, as was his habit on such occasions, he had bent the elbow vigorously. Up till then he'd been working almost every day and was a pleasure to be with, but when the sauce flowed he became somewhat hard to handle.

On this occasion, Marvin was certain we didn't have enough extras for the battle sequence. He had therefore decided in his drunken wisdom to dress himself as an extra and go on board ship to lend his assistance. 'Lee, hold on please. We can't have you on the ship – you're supposed to be somewhere else in the movie. If the camera picks you out it'll screw the film up!'

He thought about this for a moment then said, 'I'll bend over like this –' here he nodded a bit too hard and I had to prop him up '– and no one will know it's me. It'll be OK.'

'Lee, it really isn't necessary...'

But he wouldn't let me finish and eyeballed me from mean, rheumy eyes. 'Tony, you're a good kid, but, if you don't get out of my road, I'll bust your chops.'

I looked at that large, tough man and realised that, if I hit him, I could damage the priceless face and screw the next day's filming, and, if he hit me, it could cause severe damage to my face, which I prized greatly. So, feigning a change of opinion, I said, 'You're right, Lee. Maybe they could use another sailor.'

I moved to step aside, but, before I could, he grabbed me in a bear hug and kissed me. As he marched off to the ship, I called ahead to the director on the walkie-talkie about their new arrival.

'That's all I fucking well need!' he replied. 'Why did you decide to send him here, you bloody lunatic?!' Such are the thanks you can expect from a colleague.

In other films I made, Vincent Price quoted poetry, Twiggy sang, as did Deep Purple and many others. Patrick Macnee, star of *The Avengers*, on which I'd worked as an assistant director, had kindly given me three pairs of beautiful, hand-made shoes when I left the show, which unfortunately were all too long and narrow. One female star had given me even more. Michael Caine and Peter Finch had taught me respect for actors and their craft. Finch, in particular, proved that you could raise hell at night and still perform brilliantly in the morning.

At my wedding he handed me a beautiful antique silver-edged mirror and said, 'You look into this mirror and what you'll see is really you, not what anyone else says is you, but what Tony Klinger bloody well is – if he's ever going to be anything worth looking at in any event!'

So by the time I finally met The Who, it had already been a long journey for me, but a good one.

4

One Of The Boys

2 NOVEMBER 1976, LONDON

It was a cold but bright day, the sun shining through the wintry sky. I'd just finished writing an outline for a couple of promotional films for tracks from Roger Daltrey's forthcoming fourth solo album *One of the Boys*, which I was hoping to go on to direct.

Before this project came up, I'd completed a musical feature called *The Butterfly Ball*. It had been a nightmare to make because the budget had been decimated by 90 per cent just prior to filming, but I'd wanted to make a full-length film so I'd decided to go ahead in any event. The picture did OK financially and, to my astonishment, even got some good reviews (to go with some shockers). What I needed now were some quick and profitable short films, and the Daltrey job fitted the bill.

I'd listened to the title track repeatedly, staring at the typewritten lyrics until my eyes watered. For me it was a song about Roger himself, about his being both streetwise and a superstar, the common man made good. My treatment played on this paradox, using images of Roger as a kind of superpunk, Teddy boy, rocker, Hell's Angel, villain and layabout to create a mood of violence, repressed sex and frustration against a backdrop of back-street London. Thirty-four locations, plus special effects, to be shot in two days for under $10,000 — I'm not saying I was inspired but I almost expected the paper I'd been writing on to stand up and applaud. I then met up with my producer, Sydney Rose, who'd engineered the project via a friend of his (and later of mine), David Courtney, who was producing the album.

David was a very successful songwriter who had discovered Leo Sayer, and together they had written many smash hits that David also produced. He had sold many millions of records with numerous artists, so he clearly had huge talent and knew what he was doing. We talked over some projects but to be frank they were all put on the back burner when The Who and Roger Daltrey came up.

Sydney was a small, rotund man with thinning hair, a winning smile and a fondness for a cigar almost as big as he was, although he'd smoke something a great deal smaller when cash flow dictated. He was the very essence of a showbiz agent, smoking cigars, wearing sunglasses in the rain and qualifying everything he said. In the business his nickname was Confidentially Sid, because he started every sentence with a variation of: 'This is strictly confidential...' The middle of a sentence would contain the words 'I'm at the crossroads...' and it would end with: 'I'll be at the following phone numbers between 3.30 and 4pm, and I'll give you a call…' I was later convinced that somehow Woody Allen must have met Sydney and based his *Broadway Danny Rose* on an Americanised version of him.

In a strange coincidence, Sydney had once worked for my dad as a nightclub photographer, when I was a little kid. But Sydney's main experience was as an agent and he had worked for MAM, who had at one time represented and managed both Tom Jones and Engelbert Humperdinck, among others. They were a hugely powerful company at that time and this is where Sydney had learned his trade.

Sydney, who was a nice straight guy trying to make a living, thought he could put this deal together with Daltrey and Bill Curbishley, The Who's manager. This is the moment where I'm supposed to write, 'Little did I know where that would lead…' but I'll only do it on condition you realise I know I'm being a cliché. So, little did I know where that would lead – straight into the crapper!

Despite Sydney's assurances that we were on course, I couldn't help but get anxious as two weeks passed without anything more than phone calls between Daltrey's people and us. By then I'd had time to amend my treatment to cover the whole album for a documentary I'd tentatively called *Electric Sound Sandwich*, since I had always been fascinated by how an album was recorded and mixed. The story outline had gone into the black hole that seemed to surround all megastars – no reaction and dead silence. I wanted to have faith but I was having to pay the bills for my growing family and my office, and faith only takes you so far.

After another couple of weeks, in early December, Sydney rang me with some news. Dave Courtney had just telephoned him to say we were to meet Daltrey at the studio that evening to discuss ideas. We were on! At last I felt I could get excited.

After 15 minutes waiting in the messy ex-church that now served as Ramport, The Who's studio, I was getting a lot less excited. It was in Battersea, a part of London that had seen better days. Some scruffy and laconic twit of indeterminate sex asked us to wait a little longer and gave us some coffee in suspiciously dirty mugs. I quickly realised the mugs looked better than the coffee tasted – instant poison, I thought. The reception area looked like one of those 'before the paint job' advertisements. You felt like the seat you were sitting in was alive and well and crawling up your back. You could find nicer toilets.

Eventually we were told, 'Roger can see you now,' and we walked through.

The studio itself was very plush, especially compared to the khazi serving as a reception. Waiting for us were Daltrey, Courtney and some of those mysterious people who always seem to be hanging around stars, massaging egos, carrying tea and generally brown-nosing, but doing very little else.

Daltrey looked at me with those hard blue eyes. 'What are you gonna rip me off for?' they seemed to say, despite the infectious grin in that chiselled face. We said our hellos and I noticed the firmness of his handshake, a working man's grip not a limp showbiz poser's. A kind of liking for the man started in me for his direct, no-nonsense manner and it has never left me. Sometimes his directness can be disconcerting, particularly in those days when he was more rough-edged, but he's a man who calls a spade a shovel and you either get on with it or leave the building.

While Sydney and Dave chatted, I looked around the studio and noticed a big pile of film equipment on the floor by the wall.

Then Daltrey spoke to me. 'Dave here reckons we can do some stuff together, Tony. What ideas have you got?'

'I sent them to Bill Curbishley a couple of weeks back. Didn't you get them?'

He ignored this and instead said, 'Why don't you play them a couple of the tracks, Dave?'

Courtney nodded to a tape operator who pressed the play button, drowning out any possible further conversation in a sea of pulsing rock which I recognised as a final version of 'One of the Boys'. This was different, more direct; gutsy, raw edges that had grated on the ear in the demo were now trimmed, but the overall impact was even greater. It was good, very good.

'Well?' Daltrey asked me as the final sounds faded away.

'It's the best solo thing you've done, Roger,' I answered honestly.

Sydney Rose agreed. By now, everyone, bar Roger, Dave, Sydney and myself, had been asked to go and we were all sitting down in the leather swivel chairs. After we'd been given a fresh cup of tea by the laconic twit, Daltrey said, 'I'll bet you're wondering what all this film gear's doing all over the place.'

'It had crossed my mind,' I replied.

'If you've got a question, you'll learn it's best to be direct. That's how I was brought up in Acton,' he said.

'I was also brought up in Acton,' I said, 'and what is all that film gear doing here anyway?'

For the first time since we'd met, Roger genuinely smiled. 'I didn't know you came from fucking Ackers, Klinger.'

I'd obviously scored a big point and Roger did look much more pleasant when he smiled.

'I've got some kids from the film school doing some filming of me doing this album. I don't know if any of it's gonna be any good though; they don't know which end's up!'

'Is it anything like that *Electric Sound Sandwich* idea I gave Bill for you?' I asked.

'Yeah.' Roger's smile now became fixed and hard. 'A bit like that, only these guys are cheaper.'

I shifted in my seat under Sydney's anxious scrutiny. He obviously didn't want me saying the wrong thing and possibly screwing up a big opportunity, but I'd already discovered that life's too short to worry about every word you say. 'Yeah, Roger,' I said, 'but, you know, when you pay peanuts, you get monkeys!'

He seemed to appreciate my frankness, if not my target. 'Yeah, well, let's talk a bit more about your promo ideas,' he said, closing the subject emphatically.

Soon we were discussing dates, availability and, most

convincing of all, money. Daltrey came out with a torrent of suggestions and ideas in a way I later found was his usual manner. He is a man of almost limitless energy – his physical fitness was vibrant and even his hair seemed to possess electricity. He was possessed by an obsession to act – he'd fallen in love with the idea and it overwhelmed him.

'Pete doesn't wanna tour,' he told me. 'Keith's out of it altogether in California and John's happy enough doing nothing, so what am I gonna do except act? And no one offers me anything important so I'm gonna do it all myself. I'm not gonna rot waiting for something to happen with the group. It isn't a group unless we tour and make records, is it? And if the label pushes too hard, I'll fulfil my contract by recording 40 minutes of me farting. The contract just requires a Roger Daltrey album – it doesn't say what's gotta be on it, does it?'

He paused as we laughed at the idea of Roger mooning stereo microphones in splendid and expensive isolation.

'I'm not into doing the solo rock-star bit. It's bad for the ego; if it doesn't work, you're crushed. If it does work, you become such a bloody bighead you can never do anything normal again. You don't know how hard it was acting a part like Tommy, but it was something new, different – know what I mean?'

It was strange to learn so much about one of rock'n'roll's great stars so quickly. Perhaps I'd just walked in on the right night; perhaps I was still sufficiently a stranger at this stage for him to open up to me.

While we were saying our goodbyes and arranging to

meet again immediately after the holidays, he told me of the last time he'd seen Jimi Hendrix. 'He came to my house and I'd just finished varnishing all the wood floors. He goes over to a wet bit and plants his hands right in it – leaves two great paw marks. I said, "What are you up to, you berk?" He says that I shouldn't cover up the marks because soon he'll be dead and that bit of floor will be worth a fortune.'

'What did you do?' I asked.

Daltrey shrugged his shoulders. 'Well, I didn't know he was gonna kick the bucket so I varnished right over the marks.'

5

A Meeting Has Been Arranged

11 FEBRUARY 1977

By this time I had worked on setting up another film project as it was becoming clear to me that we weren't going to work with Daltrey or The Who, despite numerous reassuring phone calls from their office people. But there was still a lingering hope in me that we would soon be dancing to the rock-film beat, and I'd been trying to hang back on less interesting work when I was called by Sydney to say that a meeting had been arranged for us with Bill Curbishley, at Trinifold, one of The Who's companies, based in Soho's Wardour Street, to talk about not only promotional films with Roger but also a much more interesting possibility – a feature film with and about The Who, with yours truly directing. I'd been waiting a long time to try to make a definitive rock movie and here might be that chance.

My blood started to race and I let out a yell of sheer joy.

Now I'd have the opportunity to show what I could do given the right budget and schedule. I was like a boxer who has felt ready for a championship bout for too long. I didn't need or want any more rehearsals.

Wardour Street is London's answer to Hollywood and also has its share of pimps, hustlers and sharks. Trinifold, the Who's building, has an almost furtive entrance tucked away in an alleyway by a perpetually busy car park. You ring an entryphone and a laconic twit clears your entrance, then you shuffle up a narrow staircase, which is in no danger of appearing in *Office Beautiful*. When you get upstairs, you entered a long, narrow reception area with a beat-up, once-fashionable sofa propping up the art deco wall sporting the usual 'Look at me, I'm a successful rock act' posters and memorabilia. More interesting to me was the dishy receptionist, who offered us a coffee, 'because Bill asked me to tell you he'll be held up a few minutes and asked you to wait'.

After nearly an hour, I was getting very pissed off with Mr Curbishley and had asked the tasty secretary to tell her boss that we were waiting at least three times. Sydney, who has the patience of a saint, kept me in my seat.

Eventually, we were ushered into his presence and here we were with the man who was managing one of the most successful rock bands in the world. The older brother of former Charlton Athletic and West Ham manager Alan, Bill Curbishley is the stereotypical shrewd, hard-nut Cockney boy made good. More than six feet tall, well built and balding, he has the face of a boxer but his looks hide a brain that is sharp, very sharp indeed. Now he led us from his spartan office to a smaller, cosier room full of overstuffed white sofas, which Sydney and I sat on, and a solitary black leather armchair, where our host placed himself. His manner was brusque and abrupt to the point of rudeness. 'You wanna make a promo of Roger? Why should I let you?'

Great opening line, but, before I could launch into a counter-attack, Sydney was in the fray, quietly pointing out our previous track records and telling Curbishley that it was Daltrey who wanted us, not the other way around. As soon as that was made clear, Curbishley turned on the friendliness. His change of manner, I later realised, was caused by fear of any direct confrontation with the band. Although he was their manager, Townshend and/or Daltrey made the major decisions. Bill made the point that he was effectively the fifth member of the band more than the manager, and that's how they all preferred it.

Bill asked me what cost figure I would put on a documentary-type feature on The Who. I said I didn't know for sure, but would guess about $250,000, if it were kept simple. He said that the boys in the band could finance something of that size and keep any profit it made. He then asked if I would write up an outline treatment, and I offered to have it in his hands by the end of the month at the latest.

Although I was naturally flattered and delighted to be asked about making such a film, I was also intrigued to know their motivation for doing it. 'Is there any particular reason for making that film now, Bill?'

He smiled and thought about his reply. 'Yeah, celebrate 15 years of The Who, and maybe to say goodbye for posterity. Who knows, it could get them back on the road again, where they should be.'

It was then arranged for me to meet Daltrey again to discuss the promo films. I drove to the quiet and discreet hotel rendezvous and parked my car, which in London is an achievement sure to make your day. I vividly remember my discomfort walking past the snooty doorman and across the thick pile carpet of the foyer in my sneakers and Levis, and his knowing look of disdain when I asked, 'Which floor can I find Mr Daltrey on, please?'

Following his directions, I soon arrived at Roger's suite.

'Hello, Tony. I won't be long. I'm finishing up an interview here. Like some wine? Pour yourself one.'

I sat at the white coffee table and looked around the suite. It was a typical luxury suite, with white shag carpet, red trim, matching curtains and serviettes. You know the style – super-posh McDonalds gone mad. Daltrey was being interviewed by a high-class young lady who was trying to be working class and even managing to drop the odd 'h' in empathy with her subject, who never manages to pick one up. Their question and answer session was boring to overhear but, from all the empty coffee cups and wine glasses on the big table where they sat, I guessed they had been jabbering on for quite some time.

After about a half an hour, he ushered the girl out and we said our hellos. He poured me some more white wine and again we discussed his new album, *One of the Boys*. He then asked me which songs I didn't like, which I thought was an unusual start. I told him generally I thought the album was good and stood a very fair chance of selling well. He said that some friends of his weren't keen on a couple of the ballads and he was considering replacing them.

We then got on to the meat of our discussion, which was the album's title track. Roger asked me what my further ideas were. I told him I wanted to take the lyrics and rhythm of his song and build a mini-feature film around it. He then asked for specifics and reminded me he'd like to tie the promo to the album cover, which showed a rear view of him looking into a large mirror, microphone behind his back, but somehow the reflection was the same as the viewer saw. The rear cover showed the microphone flying through it, breaking the image. This tied in with the title track, which for me involved Roger's persona in many different guises singing into the mirror before smashing it with a microphone. I would cut between the studio and many different locales, telling the story of this street kid's anger.

He questioned me for another hour in detail and was apparently pleased with the whole project because he told me to make all the arrangements, both financial and dates, etc., with his assistant Chris, who worked at Trinifold. It occurred to me I was going to be busy finalising shooting arrangements at the same time as preparing the treatment for The Who project, which we'd agreed to call *The Kids Are Alright*, named after an early song of theirs.

Earlier in the year I'd been commissioned to do a project by John Coletta, manager of Deep Purple. I'd made two films for them, *Deep Purple Rises Over Japan* and *The Butterfly Ball*, and John had asked me to make a retrospective on the band, going back over their eight years. We'd got quite deeply into conceptual discussions when he and the group parted company, but I'd been left with some very useful notes and research on how to make a big documentary on a rock group, including old film clips wherever they could be found and how to obtain clearances for them.

I was convinced that you could only make a commercially and artistically valid rock film if you showed the individuals who made up the group and underscored their wit, humour and anarchy by putting them in situations or creating set pieces in which they could feel at ease and be shown at their best – in other words, play to the group's strengths, not weaknesses. In this context, you'd never distance the groups from their fans by emphasising their financial dealings to the exclusion of a good song. I'd always got my rocks off having a top rock act play for my cameras; speaking was usually their second-best talent. I had no reason to suppose the audience for this kind of movie would be any different. One last thing to be avoided at all costs was the word 'documentary', which at that time meant instant box-office death according to conventional film wisdom.

So I already had a dossier of notes and thoughts on how I'd like to make my rock'n'roll movie. All I'd have to do would be start my in-depth research on The Who. I suppose I was taking a lot for granted but I already knew enough about how groups operated to realise that the only way you could survive and prosper was to prepare for all eventualities. So, for your edification and delight, here is the first version of my treatment for *The Kids Are Alright*, which gives you an idea of what our venture was supposed to become…

6

The Concept

'KIDS ARE ALRIGHT'
A CONCEPT BY TONY KLINGER
COPYRIGHT TONY KLINGER, FEBRUARY 1977

THE IDEA

When one examines the history of popular music of our recent past, one coherent group stands out as an enduring entity – that group is The Who.

Why they remain while others have faded into obscurity is, of course, a matter of conjecture until the time at which they are asked how this has happened.

Whether by accident or design, remain they have, without a change in personnel or even more important a lessening of audience identification and appeal. They still are an around-the-world smash – why?

That the music is exciting, beautifully conceived, excellently produced is so obvious that I only mention it here because I am a fan endeavouring to retain objectivity.

No, more than rock is involved. Somehow The Who epitomise my generation's growing up – the revolution in attitudes of thought in regards to institutional authority to the very clothes on our back – the way we look at past values and at each other all have been transformed in the years since The Who came together.

From the days of Mods and Rockers through greasers, skinheads, angels and flower power, The Who have endured and flourished always managing to produce the sound and impact necessary to stay ahead of trends. Naturally, for weren't the group growing alongside their audience?

Therefore, we have two stories in one when we make our film – first there is the word of The Who and then there is what's happened to the world.

Looking at today's 'Punk Rock' burgeoning stars and one sees a pale, sick imitation of what The Who originated – their violence of presentation is genuine, growing out of a determination to impact us with the power of an idea in sound. It is a demand to be listened to – not just to say something to a mindless audience.

THE METHOD

We want to show more than just a collage of carelessly slapped-together memories – what we are filming is dynamite, ready to blow, our treatment must then be dynamic – how?

1) Available to us are many hours shot on the group by a confusing multitude of different film and television

directors over an ever-evolving period of turbulent change
in all the countries — this must be a great and unique
opportunity to see how the group has been visualised by
others as well as by themselves.

The intercutting techniques must blend into the current
material we will shoot and not become a glorified
'supersonically top pop show' — this film is about people
first, then what those people are into — which is great music.

2) It's my wish, artistically, to treat the better material
from the past with respect and where possible not chop it
about gratuitously.

However, when something is found which may be
considered delightfully awful, that too will be used by me.
Something that at the time of its inception was
embarrassing can become a treasure retrospectively.

Also I detect from speaking with Roger that the group has
that very rare and valuable quality — an ability to laugh with
the world at themselves.

3) Some of the past footage when transferred from its
original master material will look grainy. Without
detracting from the overall quality look of the film, I will
want to include this stuff without dressing it up. Put bluntly,
we have to be authentic both in our concept and the way we
carry it out.

OUTLINE OF WHAT WE'LL SHOOT AND WHY

A) IT IS IMPERATIVE TO FILM EACH MEMBER OF THE BAND IN THEIR OWN SURROUNDINGS

This will give us an insight into what value they might or might not place on possessions and, more importantly, why they live as they do and, in certain instances, why someone like Roger stays here and pays his taxes when he could easily leave the country to stew in its own juice.

B) THE BAND RECORDING ITS NEXT ALBUM

Obviously, in a movie of this nature, we must contain within it not only past and present music, but the future ongoing excitement as well.

Secondly, there's one hell of a lot of fans who buy albums, who have no conception of the blood, sweat and tears their idols have poured into them.

C) A MAJOR INDOOR CONCERT

Basically, the reasons for needing to film this section are twofold:

(i) It is imperative to obtain the band's new act performed before a live audience. We must see the interaction as new numbers are played and tested in the living cauldron.

(ii) Secondly, we have a controllable sound system and equally predetermined lighting rig. This means we have one live venue where we will have ideal sounds and visuals with a limited amount of technical aggro. It is essential to see The

Who play live because their roots lay in this sphere and in which they still remain supreme.

D) INTERVIEWS

There are several methods employed today in the technique of the interviewer. One can shoot head and shoulders shots answering questions commonly called vox pops – to me this is an aberration – one that contradicts the basic premise of film, which is that both the interviewee and the camera operator can and must move. Therefore, I feel that when we do interview someone it must be as unself-conscious and natural as possible and not a staged set piece.

This can only happen once the group and I know and understand each other well enough for them to lose any lingering inhibitions about opening their minds up to scrutiny. I propose not trying to grab any interviews until my crew have become part of the furniture, more or less an extension of the group itself.

I will put my questions to the men of the band from off camera and without giving them advance notice of what they'll be asked. I will not enquire into their favourite colour or material of that nature as I for one would not be able to convey that kind of information, as I feel it's irrelevant, immaterial and banal.

I want to speak to the group collectively and individually in different settings, whether the mood is upbeat or otherwise.

The type of questions I ask will sometimes be seen as lunatic in themselves but you must understand that I know all the film's component parts and where each piece fits into the jigsaw.

E) Apart from Entwistle, Moon, Townshend and Daltrey, the other people behind the scenes who run the office are almost legends in their own right. To discover what they contribute to the entity we know as The Who could be both interesting and enlightening.

This sequence should be shot during normal working hours and, if possible, with much activity contrasting with the somewhat languid image middle-aged suburbia has of such people. It would be a pleasant change to briefly put into history the theory that we in the entertainment world are a bunch of idle layabouts. Being puritanical for a moment, I believe that if you work hard you're almost bound to play hard. The Who epitomise both sides of this equation.

F) Specifics
Daltrey: I would enjoy speaking with Roger about how he sees his future both as a member of The Who and individually as a solo artist. Are the two things incompatible or is one purely an extension of the other? In relation to his acting, is this a field he wouldn't like to see blossom or did he find the thespian's discipline an invigorating experience that stretched him in new directions?

Townsend: is a man whose energies both as a composer and a performer seem endless. What motivates him forward to new things? I believe from questions I've already asked that he feels a need to express ideas in music that tell a story within which lies an analogy of life as he sees it. Simultaneously, the music which serves as the springboard for the lyrics is in itself interesting to me as it seems without exterior source, a creation totally unique and individual. Why?

It is of extreme importance to find out why Peter kicked drugs and whether he feels better or worse as a result.

ENTWISTLE: is a man of some mystique. Seemingly more self-contained as an individual than most people, he still manages to write excellent material.

Sometimes called the quiet one of the group. I would be interested to hear his opinion of his colleagues' admitted excesses on occasion. And what influence, if any, black magic and mysticism played in his musical insight. It was something that concerned me about many of the English bands of the time.

MOON: What the hell can I say about Moon...

Apart from being pretty damn good on the drums, is the boning-about part of the man or a superimposition brought about by years of heady publicity and success? I feel he's supercharged with an abnormal zest for life. Perhaps sometimes bored by people or surroundings he explodes. Whatever else he does, though, he makes people happy and that must be good. I hope to find from Keith what the more serious side feels on a variety of issues including his own rationale of his lifestyle.

G) The Group

Aesthetically speaking, this group created what I believe to be a whole new field, the rock opera. With *Tommy* a phenomenon was born, not just another album. Statistically, I'm aware of its vast sales both as a series of albums and as a movie – but what did it mean to the group? The knowledge that millions idolise them must alter their sense of perspective. Is this assertion correct?

From my objective analysis of the group as personally unknown individuals, it amazes me that four such contrary people have stayed together. Someone once said of them, 'I'm pretty sure they don't like each other – but they certainly do love each other!' It's my job to indicate the truth of this on film, either partly or completely.

H) A Major Outdoors Concert

After the build-up, this must come as the climax of our movie, an enormous explosion of colour and power as the kids in the vast audience get their chance to join with The Who in a celebration by music of the Queen's Silver Jubilee.

Backstage the artists arrive surrounded by a covey of acolytes and other stars all charged by the energy of the occasion.

The nerves build up until the point at which the audience and their heroes can mutually expend them by the performance which hopefully will include the use of the extraordinary hologram images allied to The Who's spectacular stage performance.

I) In Conclusion

The film should end with an upbeat note emphasising the mutual feelings of loyalty between fan and group. I believe 'My Generation' or 'Long Live Rock' both do this and we'll choose which comes out right. The fans deserve it!

7

The Plan

Sydney Rose and I grabbed a cab from my office to Trinifold and, unusually, Bill didn't keep us waiting more than a few minutes. We entered his office and he asked us whether we'd ever seen the movie *Tommy*. We both had, sometime previously, but said we'd like to again. Then he asked me what thoughts I had come up with on making a film about The Who.

I had been doing some heavy research just for this question and had found so much potential material that I didn't know where to start. For me, the seminal Who record at the time was still *Live at Leeds* and the best archive visuals had to be from the Monterey and Woodstock festivals. They were great and the career of the band – in fact, the face of youth culture – hinged on these moments for me. At that time (1969), *Tommy* had drifted down the American album charts, but after the Woodstock festival it rocketed back up, and was to do so again after the film came out in 1975. I was also fascinated and amused by Townshend's following of the Indian mystic Meher Baba, and wanted to know more. Not to take the piss, but because I thought it was one of the things about him that informed and influenced his soul and therefore his musical output.

I outlined my plans to Bill and he liked them. He asked me how long it would take to prepare a complete scenario, budget and schedule. I said that I could finish by the end of the week. As I'd emphasised research of material so heavily, he told us about a big fan of the band from New York, Jeff Stein, who, on his own accord, had done a lot of research work locating material in many countries. Bill didn't know how good or accurate the kid's work was, but, if it could help us when and if we got going, it was available.

I responded enthusiastically. Could I see the material? Meet Stein? Maybe he could be the film's researcher? It was obvious to me that, if his research was any good, it could save the project months of work and a small fortune on the budget.

Bill told me to get my work done and we'd see how far things went. We set a dinner date for the 25th and following that we'd discuss my ideas more fully, and he'd get us a private screening of *Tommy* at the Audley Square Theatre in Mayfair.

The next couple of days were full of hectic activity as I worked on polishing and revising my treatment. Next, I drafted a rough schedule and from this a working production budget. Bill had asked me for a firmer ball-park guesstimate of the film's cost, but it was a bit like being asked how long is a piece of string.

At the same time, I was still furiously researching and collecting material about the band. For me the most interesting person was clearly Townshend, but the most fun on screen was surely going to be Moon. He was electric on stage and in person, and his drumming reflected his personality – larger than life, manically energetic, theatrical, funny, crashing, bashing and hugely expressive of his expansive talents. More than his crazed behaviour, the thing I first thought about when I considered Moon was that he was one of the greatest rock drummers ever. The speed of his playing, the invention and the irreverence set him apart. Daltrey described this very well, with Pete and John being the two knitting needles and Keith being the ball of wool. You couldn't take Keith out of it unless you wanted the band to simply sound confused and in pieces. Unlike most drummers, he consistently switched from the more simple rhythms to play along with the vocals, and this was his genius.

But Keith wasn't just the drummer, he was the soul of the band, and we had to catch this on film for our movie to work. Keith was the first rock drummer to become the centre of attraction in a band, and he was the irrepressible driving energy behind The Who. Without him the band would have probably been too dark to succeed. He brought them some lightness and humour and fun.

I wasn't sure if we should bring up any issues about drugs as this did form part of the story of The Who. They had all started out with speed, amphetamines, except for Roger who was clean. At the other end of the spectrum was Keith who, initially, always went further than the others. When someone else might have taken one or two purple hearts, Keith could consume 20 in one hit and then go on stage and play wonderfully well, if too fast!

I estimated that we'd spend something like half a million dollars, depending on my being able to direct and edit as I saw fit, with Sydney keeping a tight day-to-day hold on the accounts. If we played at it, we'd have a very expensive home movie. Bill had agreed that he wanted talented professionals to run the picture and, furthermore, provisionally accepted a budget in the range I'd suggested. He told us that the money to finance the film would be coming from The Who, and that he would watch over every penny spent on behalf of their company, Rock Films.

When we finished our preparations, we decided to see Bill sooner than arranged. Subtly, our relationship changed at this stage. We'd been demoted in his eyes from colleagues to employees. At best this would work uneasily; at worst it would become impossible. But because I could envisage glory and dollar bills I refused to believe all the warning signals.

In retrospect I believe this change in Bill came about because, in his heart, he wanted to be a film producer and that was to lead us into many problems. Our conversations at this early stage became a learning experience for Curbishley, another problem on which I didn't place enough emphasis. How would I control a situation in which I was going to be second-guessed by an understandably self-interested group of individuals who in the last resort could pull the plug on our project financially at any time they chose?

If I'd have known what it was going to be like to juggle the band's hair-trigger egos while blindfolded by an ambitious manager, I'd never have gone into another meeting. That foresight escaped me. All I had was an uneasy churning in the gut – not bad enough, mind you, to walk out on thousands of pounds, so, still feeling I could control both my gut and the project, I worked on.

After examining all our paperwork, Bill said he was going to distribute it to the group with his firm recommendation. He told us that, except for technical details, we had a deal. In essence, I was to write, direct and supervise editing. Sydney would produce and Bill would act in the band's best interest.

I was a very successful, highly paid and extremely contented young man. I was 26 years old and I already had a beautiful family, a four-bedroomed house, the obligatory sports car, money in the bank and sublime faith in my own talent. When it's good and is coming at you from every direction, you somehow believe there's only one way to go – and that's up. I knew I was lucky to be doing just what I loved and getting paid handsomely for doing it, but then I'd never encountered much else since I'd made my first small films when I was 19. I'd always taken risks and usually had landed feet first. You have to be talented and lucky, but, above all, hardworking and ambitious to get anywhere in the entertainment world, or any other.

So I was 26 and winning, with all that entailed, such as a

king-sized, easily bruised ego, tunnel vision and a failure to care about other people. If you gave the other guy an even break, he might just stomp all over your face. One thing I've learned about myself between then and now is that I had and still have a great deal to learn.

The next evening, Sydney and I met Bill Curbishley and his wife, Jackie, for the *Tommy* screening and afterwards we had dinner. The restaurant's atmosphere was friendly if a touch self-consciously trendy. A lot of well-known faces from the gossip columns were there, munching their way through their expense accounts. We learned that Daltrey and Entwistle were already keen to go ahead as quickly as possible. Moon was looning about somewhere in California and Townshend was working in private on demos for a new album by the group.

Bill asked me every conceivable question on my ideas for making and selling the film. It was more like an interrogation than a chat. Although we were the people who were being hired to make the movie, it felt like an audition in reverse, since Bill was intent on telling us how much of *Tommy* he'd been responsible for. I was getting more nervous about Curbishley with every meeting.

Bill explained to us in the strictest confidence that he had big plans for himself and The Who in the film industry. They believed in the motion-picture industry, and in particular the British end of it, and therefore they were acquiring a few stages at the venerable Shepperton Film Studios in Middlesex, some land by the River Thames and the grand old house that had served as the office building during the halcyon days of the British film industry. I was pleased that the band were showing such obvious interest in the future of films, particularly British films.

During this period of expansive conversation, Bill described some of the subjects they were keen to make into future films. Townshend had a project called *Lifehouse*, which at that time was an obscure and brief idea. Daltrey had just purchased the film rights to an autobiography by John McVicar, a British criminal with whom Roger strongly identified. I had read the book at Roger's urging and found it fascinating. My reservations, which I later expressed to Roger, were primarily centred on making a film for the world market about a Cockney tough guy who, by dint of his own intellect and hard work, had made himself into an eloquent spokesman for the prison population. I felt it was too parochial to stand any chance in the American market unless it turned out as an artistic masterpiece, which is something that happens very occasionally but which you certainly can't bank on.

Bill also told me of his plans to turn *Quadrophenia*, the band's sixth album from 1973, into a film. Again, I expressed some reservations because I couldn't see it as a film doing well outside of certain north European countries, especially England. Later, I was pleased to see both *Quadrophenia* and *McVicar* were produced but they didn't do very well internationally, although I enjoyed both. This move into the film world by the band was to be preceded by our project as a costly experiment, learning experience and springboard to legitimate filmmaking.

Bill's compulsion to diversify the band's activities and

investments out of purely musical avenues was further evidenced by their large-scale investments in lasers, holographs and trucking. Bill told us about John Woolf, a technical genius who ran their laser and holographic enterprises. At his direction, the band poured a fortune into this field of endeavour with brilliant technical success. Later, I saw an exhibition of this advanced work at a London gallery and I've seen nothing to compare with it.

It was clear that the band's emphasis was shifting to visual media. Bill's mood as he told us about their plans was infectious and enthusiastic. The dinner, which had started with us all being stiff and formal, had relaxed to the point where we swapped anecdotes and jokes while the coffee was poured. Bill told me more about his close involvement with all aspects of the *Tommy* film production and it was clear he felt his efforts should have been more visibly acknowledged. It was also soon obvious that an integral part of The Who's plans for their films would be the words 'Producer: Bill Curbishley' – if not at once, then very soon. Bill evidently saw himself deeply involved in film production. The fact he really knew nothing about making films never deterred him for a moment.

Before we parted, it was arranged to meet again in a few days to assess the treatment and all the attached material. Bill informed us that Jeff Stein's research work included a 20-minute reel of film clips and interviews that he'd managed to gather together over the previous couple of years. But it was also becoming clear that, whoever this Jeff Stein guy was, Curbishley didn't like him one little bit. After a last-ditch concentrated effort, I handed over all the final paperwork for *The Kids* towards the end of February. Bill phoned me later in the day to say it looked good and that he was having copies made for immediate distribution to the band.

As the weeks passed by, we got more phone calls but no contracts. We'd spent months working towards what now seemed like a phantom project. After all, they had been the ones who had suggested a start date for production of late May. Now March had come and gone without any sign of action. Trying to pin anyone down, even for a definite 'no go', was impossible. Sydney and I agreed to prepare as if it would come together on the agreed dates, so that if it did we'd be ready. We were taking a huge risk by doing this. If The Who backed out, Sydney and I could be left with a $100,000 cancellation cost. But, if we didn't take the risk of preparing crews, equipment, facilities, offices, staff, laboratories, etc., there simply wouldn't be time to do it later. It was frustrating and worrying.

In April, Roger and I met again, very calmly as if our last meeting had only been a day previously. He set the 21st and 22nd of the month to shoot the promotional short for 'One of the Boys', but he also confirmed that the budget, script and schedule for *The Kids Are Alright* were fine and was keen as mustard to get going. I admit I was surprised at this happy turn of events.

I was in for more surprises when we later met Bill for lunch. He gave us a total green light on *The Kids*. The band had approved everything. They'd even added a few thousand dollars to the budget to pay Jeff Stein something for the research he'd already done. Bill said this figure was for him to negotiate directly with Stein. I was so happy I almost let the feeling of Bill's increasing anxiety about Stein slip by me.

Within two weeks, everything was set and on 21 April we began the shoot for 'One of the Boys'. Day one was at Lee's Studios, which then were in Shepherds Bush, West London, and, after we'd set up a complicated mirror shot so that Roger could sing to the playback tape in all his different guises, we were ready to start photography by 8.30am.

Roger appeared first in punk gear for that section of our film. He looked good, but immediately took issue with the way I'd situated the camera behind him. I was going to shoot his face in the mirror, which was naturally towards the camera. That way I could smash his reflection, which would disorient the viewer, who would have assumed he was watching the action head on. But Roger had no liking for standing with his back to the camera. Instant confrontation. 'I didn't know I was supposed to stand this way round. I'm not going to stand here like a ponce, the wrong way round,' he stated emphatically.

I tried to talk to him quietly, one to one. I believe you should handle things quietly on the set, but Roger wasn't having any of my peace-making. 'You'd better bloody well change your plans, Klinger. This doesn't make any sense to me.'

I could feel the crew's eyes and ears on me, waiting for the reaction. Whoever wins confrontations like this on the first set-up of a shoot invariably controls things from then on. 'I've been hired by you guys to direct, Roger, but, if you want to do it, you're welcome. I'll go home and you get on with it.'

I turned to leave, but felt Roger's hand on my arm. 'OK, I'll go along with your way, Tony, but it better turn out right.' He finished with a smile on his face and took up his position before the cameras. The tension evaporated and the crew almost audibly let out their collective breath.

For two days, we filmed amicably and efficiently across the back streets of London, and in doing so we gained one another's respect for each doing our jobs properly and with enthusiasm. Roger seemed to be at his happiest in heavy make-up and costume, and, from a director's standpoint, he was a delight to have before the camera. Our film's leading lady was a really gorgeous, well-endowed woman called Maddy Smith. Once Roger saw her, his pursuit of her on camera was a delight. He even forgot to drink so much tea. When we'd finished shooting, I cut the film myself.

It was one of those times when something I'd planned turned out just right. MCA in America and Polydor Records everywhere else were releasing Roger's album and they, along with Curbishley and Daltrey, were seemingly delighted with the clip. I'm told that in the US it was played on the *Star Wars* bill and on innumerable TV stations. It was, by any measure, a success. If this was any guideline, I allowed myself to think, then filming *The Kids Are Alright* would be easier than I'd anticipated.

After the shoot, Daltrey invited Sydney and me to his Sussex mansion for lunch. Once there we discovered that he didn't eat very much, nor stretch to much in the way of hospitality. For lunch we had lukewarm tea and a packet of wholewheat chocolate biscuits between us. Our hunger notwithstanding, I was impressed by the enormous house and large grounds, which Roger proudly showed to us. But the overriding impression it left was that the sheer size of the place overwhelmed the furniture and the people. We got into a conversation about possessions when I asked Roger about his helicopter.

'Oh, that's a bit of fun,' he said. 'I rent it out from Battersea when I'm not using it myself. They only cost £60,000 to $70,000 second hand, you know. It's a bloody good tax write-off. You should get one, Tony.'

It was said with such simple sincerity that I didn't have the heart to say I couldn't because I didn't have the money.

Next Roger took us down to his private lake, which he'd just had stocked with fish that apparently he would later try to catch. Then he showed us his beautiful and expensive cars, including a new gorgeous Ferrari.

It was a spectacular collection, but I wondered how could he, or anyone else in his position, maintain his angry, deprived young man attitudes when he was so obviously relishing the material rewards of the society he was supposed to be attacking. He now embodied the establishment – perhaps not in the clothes he wore or the way he spoke, but in every other way he'd become a wealthy citizen, a pillar of society. Last and perhaps most cruel of all, I'd noticed in the close-ups that his face wasn't so young any more. Yet, for all these contradictions, I still believe Roger's angry street kid's stance was – and still is – sincere and genuine. He just doesn't see the paradox he inhabited, or perhaps he simply didn't understand it at that time.

8

Let The Negotiations Begin

Sydney and I had decided to use the same lawyer, Brian Eagles, in our contractual negotiations. So, on a crisp May morning, together with Sydney's accountant, Alan Maysing, we all trooped into a Pall Mall law firm. The place had a distinctly Dickensian ambience, as did Sam Sylvester, who acted as the band's attorney.

After the initial thrust and parry was over, we got down to business. The entire band had agreed to go ahead, and now, at last, we could get down to making our film. Curbishley, who had been quiet until now, asked me if I had a production company available, so the film could be channelled through it. Couldn't I see it up in lights? 'A Tony Klinger Production, starring The Who...'

I thought about it for all of a second. If I let my company be used as the production vehicle, what could happen if the band stopped the funding for any reason? Say they didn't

55

like something I did, or said, or just the colour of my eyes? I'd be left holding hundreds of thousands of pounds' worth of bills, all with my name on, and I'd really just be acting as an agent of the band. All that just to have my name in lights twice instead of the once I'd get anyway? Thanks a lot, but no thanks.

Bill turned his twin-barrelled glare to Sydney, who was seated to my right. 'How about you, Syd? How would you like it to be "A Sydney Rose Production"? How about using your company?'

Sydney started to nod his head in agreement, stars definitely in his eyes, so I kicked him quite hard under the table and suggested we adjourn for a moment to consider this development.

Once we were alone, I cautioned Sydney with the troubling thoughts that had crossed my mind. Brian Eagles and I were sure that anyone or any company acting as the production company would be open to tremendous financial pressure if The Who decided to pull the plug on their flow of money. Again, I warned Sydney that he was taking an unnecessary risk, but that presentation credit loomed ever larger in his mind. He decided to do it.

We returned to the conference and Sydney told Bill that he'd be pleased to use his company, Sydney Rose Productions, for the film.

After this was settled, I asked Bill why the contracts had no mention in them of the movie's soundtrack album rights. He said there wouldn't be an album from the film. I said I couldn't believe it: we'd be making a film with one of the world's biggest and best rock bands and there wouldn't be an album?

'I've just told you there won't be an album,' Curbishley replied. 'No way. Townshend's already said he doesn't want it, and neither do I!'

What could I say? If I'd pressed it further, I could have screwed the whole deal, and for what? The guy was swearing to a room full of witnesses that there wasn't going to be a record, and, if there was, he was going to give us our rightful piece, which he'd never argued against anyhow. Maybe there really wasn't going to be an album after all. And so, on that basis, we eventually did sign the papers to make the movie. I was to direct, write and edit. Sydney would be the production company and producer. Rock Film, The Who's Gibraltar company, would finance. As a point of interest, the contracts were more than five times longer than the storyline or concept for the film. But finally production would start on 30 May.

9

Live Rock

I soon began to realise I wasn't going to love The Who as much as I loved their music. When I was growing up in the 1960s, we didn't just listen to rock music, we lived it. I grew my hair way down my back, wore Cuban-heel boots, skin-tight jeans and cheesecloth or raw-silk shirts with no collars, made in India. We went to small clubs and listened to acts who focused our minds on ourselves: The High Numbers (later to become The Who), The Rolling Stones, The Beatles, and many others who have since faded into obscurity. The clubs we went to were mostly dark, sweaty, crowded and hectic. The best of all was a Soho club called The Marquee. Whoever booked the acts there was touched by some kind of genius; somehow the club continually found new, exciting talent and the place always seemed packed to the doors.

I remember, albeit vaguely, the first time I saw The Who perform at The Marquee. This was before Townshend started smashing guitars, but Daltrey did swing his mike and Moon seemed to possess unending frenetic energy as he attacked his drum kit. The Who were prototype punks, then called Mods. Much of southern England's youth was divided between Mods and Rockers. Mods dressed smartly in button-down shirts, skinny ties and thinly lapelled suits, wore their hair very short and transported themselves on Lambretta mopeds. Frustrated anger and violence were part of their existence, and The Who became their mirror image and their cult heroes.

Although anyone older than themselves was held in contempt, the Mods' main target was another tribal grouping, known as Rockers. The descendants of the 1950s Teddy boys, Rockers wore leathers when they could afford to, denim jeans and waistcoats, and motorcycle boots. They wore their hair longer than Mods, greased it back and danced to the rhythms of such figures as Jerry Lee Lewis, early Elvis Presley and Billy Fury. They drove big powerful motorbikes and their holy of holies – Rockers' heaven – was to own a well-polished Harley Davidson.

These two groups would attack each other on sight, just for the hell of it. They would also attack other youths who didn't belong to either side. I'm not describing a limited gang-war situation such as you can find today in any ghetto or rundown inner-city area. Mods and Rockers numbered in the hundreds of thousands and were like two opposing hordes, waiting to explode against one another or society at large. This was the background of early English rock music; if a group could gain the loyalty of the Mods or Rockers, they would also turn the key to instant riches.

English rock'n'roll had only been slightly coloured by

the great American precursors such as Chuck Berry; these artists were simply not a saleable commodity to England's waspish youth, who couldn't identify with them and wanted to see their own reflection on stage. Leaving school at 14 or 15, these kids had almost zero possibility of further education, unlike their more fortunate and affluent American cousins. After a brief education, most were unequipped for anything more than mind-numbing jobs on outdated production lines, leading inevitably to boredom and frustration. Relief was only found at pubs and clubs, drinking, dancing and fighting.

To understand the magnitude of this burgeoning youth counterculture, one had to witness thousands of Mods and Rockers engage in brawling rampages at some of England's famous old coastal resort towns. The whole mad violence and excitement of these tumultuous days scared and fascinated me. Despite being nervous, my fascination with these history-making events won out and, with a group of friends, all of us unaligned proto-hippies, I set off by British Railways to Brighton.

We were there for only a day and two or three times we were very lucky not to get our heads kicked in. It was like visiting Attila's hordes while they were holidaying from the scene of their usual local rampages, and the sleepy coastal resorts' police forces were totally swamped by the sheer size of the young crowds looking for any kind of excitement and trouble that could be found. Hundreds were injured in the fighting and many more arrested by the police. Townshend later used these days of turmoil as the background for *Quadrophenia*, which for me ranks as his most important film work, but that's another story.

So why did this troubled generation produce such a renaissance in art in the mid- to late 1960s? It was partly a result of mass exposure to television, which only reached every living room in Britain in that decade. Suddenly, the possibilities were visible for all to see, but there were only a few ways a working-class kid could hope to get what they saw on the box. They could steal, or they could aspire to professional sports. The first had obvious drawbacks, and the latter was extremely limited in numbers. Or you could convince some mates to form a rock'n'roll band, scrounge some primitive musical instruments and a couple of tinny amplifiers and try your luck. It had to be more fun than delivering milk or those endless, mindless production lines.

While discussing the film *McVicar* (in which he'd starred as the English villain), Daltrey himself later said that he could easily have ended up on the wrong side of the law had he not been fortunate enough to become involved in The Who. The parallels existed, but Roger's ego and machismo were satisfied by rock'n'roll not crime, although he says there's not a lot of difference – it was the same thrill of getting away from being an average grey person.

With this background as a springboard, The Who managed to build a growing army of support among the Mods; only later were they more generally supported. English rock'n'roll in the 1960s had evolved from working-class roots, but the symbols of their impact – such as Townshend's op art happenings and guitar-smashing – were almost totally contrived to gain media attention by their then management team of Kit Lambert and Chris Stamp. Townshend himself has disclosed that, after his first big guitar smash-up at a show was missed by a national newspaper's photo-journalist, he had to stage a second one later in the act for the tardy Fleet Street man – even though at that time the group couldn't pay for their equipment, let alone a new guitar for Pete every night.

But none of these contrivances detracted from the group's raw edge, which was what set them apart. Even then they were the best live act around. Although personally I liked to listen to the bluesier Rolling Stones, I loved to watch The Who play live. Pete Townshend just seemed to jump higher and stay up longer than anyone else, his arms flailing manically like windmills, and feeding his electric sound into his sound system to get feedback was all new, wonderful and exciting to me and my generation. I would have scoffed at anyone telling me that The Who's Pete Townshend broke guitars to gain media attention.

I also liked the fact that The Who didn't play *The Ed Sullivan Show* on American television, as it set them apart from the other English bands then 'invading' America. I thought they were all selling out, although for some obscure reason I was also proud that there were millions of Americans watching and listening to our English bands.

In 1967, I'd just left school and was working as a third assistant director on the television series *The Avengers*. Another decade of learning my film craft lay ahead before I would work with The Who, but that early love of rock music stayed with me. When I got my first opportunities to use music on my own faltering early documentaries, I would haunt all the London music publishing houses with my then partner, Michael Lytton, searching for unreleased rock music tracks by as yet unknown artists.

Apart from satisfying our backers, who would like anything that didn't cost a lot, we also managed to find some gems. For our film *Extremes* in 1970, for example, we managed to obtain several wonderful tracks from a bunch of starving musicians called Supertramp. The cost was £650, and for the same amount again we could have had a share in the publishing, but I didn't have the money. Years later, I played soccer regularly with some of the lads from that hugely successful band but their memory of that era seemed to have almost evaporated.

Virtually without exception, I'd make almost every deal on every rock picture, big or small, on a handshake. The contractual paperwork would follow, sometimes after the whole film had been made. This was before lawyers, agents and accountants had taken over all the business aspects of showbiz. It isn't a pleasant way of dealing but now it's the generally accepted method: instead of a handshake, you get an overly long contract that indicates only that negotiations have just begun.

In those days, I believed what people said to me because of a handshake. We may have been idealistic fools in the late 1960s and early 1970s, but there was a good spirit of hope in the air. We had principles, even if they might appear woolly in retrospect. Now the only God is money and always remember that nice guys finish last. The Who just seem to have arrived at that state of affairs sooner than most others.

10

Pulls The Strings?

Before preparations for shooting could begin, we needed money and as yet that hadn't been forthcoming. During this period, we had time to reflect on whether the band knew what was being done in their name. I wanted to phone Roger Daltrey and tell him, but in my gut I had the growing, gnawing suspicion that he, along with the other guys, must be calling the shots. After 15 years at the top, we reasoned, the band must be on the ball. To get to the top, you need luck and talent, but, to stay there, you need brains. The band had to know what was happening, so, if we were getting the runaround, one of two things was happening: either the band was short of cash, which seemed unlikely, or there was another as yet unknown problem.

We went to see Bill Curbishley. He assured us the delays were purely technical and that we could prepare to start shooting in June. By the way, did I have any further thoughts on a title or job for Jeff Stein?

I repeated that he'd been very helpful with all the research he'd already done. I also said I didn't care what he was called. 'Call him Executive Producer if it's some kind of problem.'

Bill then said we should come to a screening of the footage Stein had assembled a year or two previously and which the band had paid for. We went to see it the next day. It was a 15–20-minute collage of Who footage and, although it was obviously done on a slim budget, it had some good ideas and was well executed. Bill told us that it had cost something like $20,000, and Stein and an editor pal, Eddie Rothkowitz, had pulled it together as a labour of love from bits and pieces they'd managed to beg, steal or borrow in England and America. 'In fact,' Bill added, 'how would you feel about a situation in which you and Stein co-directed?'

My mouth must have dropped open. We'd just spent months negotiating and agreeing a deal for me to direct, and now I had to field a question like that. 'I won't co-direct,' I replied. 'I don't think you can ever get two people who don't know each other to co-direct successfully. If you want Stein, you can have him, but not me as well!'

Bill then told me and Sydney that, three or four years earlier, when Stein was a teenage Who freak following them from gig to gig across the US, he had become very friendly with Townshend who had promised him that, in the event the band ever made a film about themselves, Stein would be the director. Sydney and I must have looked like a couple of goldfish gasping for air; the whole thing was becoming a nightmare.

Curbishley carried on talking. He said that he and everyone else bar Townshend, who I'd still not met, agreed that I should direct, not Stein. Perhaps I would be the supervising director, making sure things went OK, while Stein got one camera to play with?

I said that I didn't see how all this had become my problem. I'd negotiated a contract in good faith, and I had no argument with Stein. I'd had enough and we hadn't done a single shot. I wanted out.

Bill told me not to be hasty; he'd straighten it out. I was still going to direct. He wanted me to. So did Roger. John Entwistle and Keith would go along with them. So it was only Pete Townshend and he'd see about that. As Sydney and I rose to go, he added that Stein had already arrived in London from New York and we would all get together and sort it out.

Sydney and I left and walked across the street to a coffee bar. Neither of us spoke for a while. Then Sydney dropped another bomb on me when he suggested that maybe we could both be producers and Stein could direct. I told him that I didn't want to produce films any more, and especially with an unknown quantity who I hadn't selected as the director. We'd sweated blood to get this far with our concept and now we were letting it go down the tubes without a thought for what we'd originally wanted to do – make the ultimate rock movie. There comes a point when you have to choose between making deals and making films.

The next day, we were due to set up our production offices in Pinewood Studios, in the countryside just outside London. We'd now begun the detailed planning of the first shoot, which was to be a sequence tailored around The Who playing together for the first time in over a year in rehearsal at Shepperton. We'd hired a production manager, research assistant, secretary and assistant editor, and had arranged a multi-camera crew set-up with all the necessary equipment for June, and here we were in May, not properly financed, not knowing if I'd direct or walk, and my prospective replacement was nowhere to be found. Both Sydney and I tried to arrange a meeting of the band, Stein, Curbishley and us, but we met with silence.

Sydney and I then talked it over at great length with each other and our mutual lawyer. We decided that, as we had an actual production agreement, signed by us all, we had no alternative but to carry on as if everything was normal and prepare to film. I made three crucial decisions at this stage, which on reflection still seem correct. First, I resolved to put every single thing I did or said in writing, so there'd be a record to point to if self-protection was later necessary. Second, I told Sydney that I would not sign a single cheque to anyone for anything during the production, because I had the feeling anything anyone did involving the band's money was going to be a problem later on. Last but not least, I demanded – and got – the first instalment of my fee, which was in the budget and due at that time under my contract with Sydney's production company. I made sure this payment was placed on record in the weekly financial statement, copies of which went to everyone involved. By doing this, I'd not only got myself my first money after a lot of work, but established that my contract was in effect. I saw a shooting war on the horizon and I'd donned my flak jacket.

Two weeks went by but there was still no sign of Jeff Stein. I looked around the offices, which were large, old fashioned and slightly musty, and wondered if all the preparatory work was actually going to come to anything. I'd told my wife, Avril, that if they pushed me into producing I was going to quit, and she stood by me. Sydney had become ill with worry that all his dreams were going to be grabbed from him. He'd put on a lot of weight and looked pasty and sallow. The office atmosphere was charged with electricity. We all knew the storm was going to break, we just didn't know when.

Finally, Curbishley telephoned to say he was on his way over with someone he thought we should meet, and, an hour later, he showed up with Jeff Stein in tow. Stein was young and slim, with long blond hair. He was wearing drawstring trousers and an open-necked Hawaiian-type shirt, and was carrying a suitcase and a duffel bag. We shook hands and assessed each other warily. He didn't look like much of an ogre to me. It seemed incredible that this innocuous-looking guy had so much influence over The Who.

Curbishley introduced us all. We couldn't exchange any pleasantries as Bill launched straight into a speech, telling us we'd have to sort out the whole mess about who'd direct — Stein or me, or Stein and me — because if we didn't there wouldn't be any film at all. He went on in this vein for quite a while, but it was typical carrot-and-stick stuff. Be good boys and everything will work out. If you don't do as you are told by Uncle Bill, you'll suffer hell and damnation. All of which neatly avoided the fact that he and his pals had caused the entire fuck-up in the first place.

Then came the great clincher, uttered as Bill ushered Sydney out of the room with him: 'Now I'm going to lock you two guys in this room and whoever walks out alive will be the director.' He pulled the door shut and Stein and I sat down, both reflecting on the insanity of the situation we were in.

I spoke first. 'Look, Jeff, it seems to me you and I don't have an argument. It's Bill and the band that signed contracts with both of us to direct. As far as I'm concerned, you signed first, you get it, and I'll walk away.'

Jeff got up and started to pace. He was so tense I thought he'd bust in two or cry. He turned to face me directly and his voice shook with anger. 'You tried to steal my film and now you're trying to kill it!'

I asked him what the hell he was talking about and he told me that I'd plotted to kick him out, to copy his concept and to destroy his credibility.

'Hold on,' I insisted, seeing red myself. 'Who told you that crap? I didn't know who you were or that you had a contract or even see your concept, so how could I copy it? As I just told you, I don't have a fight with you, but, if you want to start one, just carry on!'

He calmed down a bit but continued pacing to and fro, wearing the already threadbare carpet down some more. Then he stopped and spoke quietly, now like a lost child – full of sincerity, warmth, hope and compassion. 'You know they won't fund the film without you on it, don't you?'

I didn't, and I said so.

'I've been with Pete the last two weeks and he'll go with me directing,' he went on, 'but even he wants you to produce. The others insist on you being there, doing one or the other. Be reasonable. I don't mind you producing – in fact, I'd like you to produce – but, if you walk, the movie's gonna be dead.'

'I've said it a million times, but I'll say it again. I don't want to produce and I think co-directing stinks.'

'So do I!' he interjected. 'And I can't be held to blame if everyone else breaks their agreements and all I want to do is keep mine.'

'Christ! I'm even prepared to walk away and not get another penny. What else does everyone want?'

'Listen, Tony,' he replied. 'It's not such a bad deal. You'll get your fees, you'll get your percentage and a terrific credit on a Who movie – that isn't so shabby. Otherwise none of us will get a thing.'

I could see he meant it, but I'd made my mind up way before. 'No, I'm going to walk. Make Sydney your producer – he's a good guy.'

'They won't go with Sydney,' he said, which meant he'd already tried that one out for size.

'Then maybe there'll be no movie. I'm sorry for you,

Jeff, and I'm sorry for me. You seem like a nice guy but I'm not going to get screwed like this just because they're The Who. I won't take crap like this from anyone.'

He straightened up and we shook hands. As he opened the door, Sydney and Bill came in. 'Did you two sort yourselves out?' Bill asked.

'Yeah, we're gonna think it over,' said Jeff, looking at me and smiling.

'OK, but I want this finished by tomorrow morning,' Bill said, as he took Jeff out of the room.

'What happened?' asked Sydney, sitting on the grey mock-leather settee.

I told him the whole conversation and expressed my view that I just couldn't understand what had possessed the band to sign such an open-ended deal with Stein. 'I'm finished on the picture. I've told him I'll back out and you should produce but they won't wear it. Why don't you ring Roger and see if he knows what's going down?'

Sydney rang Daltrey, and, although I could only hear Sydney's end of the conversation, he was repeating snatches of what Roger replied for my benefit. 'Hello, Roger, it's Sydney ... sorry to bother you at home, but something very important has come up ... Yes, about the film ... about who's supposed to direct ... oh ... I know it's Tony as far as you're concerned, but what about Stein? ... You don't want him to direct? ... I see ... Well, he was just here with Bill and apparently he has this agreement with Peter for him to direct which Pete signed years ago ... Let me get this straight. You're saying that's Pete's problem if he signed

72

something? It doesn't bind you or the others to him? ... I'll get Tony from the other room.' At this Sydney covered the mouthpiece of the phone and whispered, 'He won't finance the film without you. Speak to him yourself.'

I took the phone and a deep breath. 'Hello, Roger.'

'Hello, Tony. Listen, can't you buggers sort this out? It's becoming a real pain, you know. Maybe we'd all be better off if it was scrubbed once and for all, but, if we are gonna do it, you've gotta be there. Did Bill tell you I said that, me and the others?'

'Yes,' I replied, 'but how's it gonna work, Roger? There can't be two directors, two camps – it'll be a real mess.'

He paused a moment. 'Listen, he can stand behind the camera and you stand behind him, make sure he points it in the right direction, gets film in it, you know? Don't get yourself into a big ego deal, Tony. You'll still be in charge. Look, don't say nothing yet. Put Sydney back on and we'll talk in an hour or two. Ta ra.'

As Sydney went into his office to continue his conversation, I sank heavily on to a chair and let the whole messy situation percolate in my head like so much stale brew. Confusion reigned supreme; somehow I'd lost control of my own fate. I'd been manoeuvred into a position where whatever I did was partly right and partly wrong, even if it meant losing money, prestige and friends. I resolved to stick to my decision to quit.

But, before I could go into Sydney's office to tell him, he came back in and staggered to the armchair. He was grey, his breath came in short gasps and he held his right hand to his chest. I told him to lie down, fetched him some water and asked him what was wrong. Had he ever had an attack like this before?

'I'll be all right in a minute,' he answered, loosening his tie and undoing his collar. 'You know they mean it, don't you?' he asked. He sat up slightly and turned to face me. 'They're not going to finance the film if you don't produce it – there'll be no film at all.'

'They've made that fairly clear,' I answered.

Sydney still seemed to be having difficulty breathing. 'They'll go with you producing,' he gasped. 'I can be executive producer and Stein will direct. Let's do it, Tony! It's not so bad. C'mon, let's do it. You're still getting your deal, I'll get mine and it'll only be for about seven or eight months.'

'Sydney, if we let them get away with this now, then there'll never be an end to what they can do. No, I don't like being taken for a fool. They're like spoiled kids. The only reason they want me this second is because they can't have me. If I do what they want, they'll soon get fed up with me and they'll want a new toy.'

'Tony, listen for a minute. We've become good mates in the last few months, haven't we?'

I nodded my head; I liked Sydney.

'If I told you something in the strictest of confidence, you'd keep it to yourself, wouldn't you?'

'Yes,' I replied. 'What is it?'

He sat forward now, his short podgy frame bent, his neat feet spread, his balding head supported on the palms of his hands, elbows balanced on knees. 'I'm at the crossroads of my life, Tony. I've got severe financial difficulties. If I don't do this film, I'm in big trouble, immediate trouble.' He looked up at me, his eyes full of tears. 'I'm not kidding – you know me better than that. I won't be able to pay the mortgage on the house. Both the kids go to private school; I've got their fees to pay. I owe the bank and they're waiting on this deal to see me through. Tony, I really need this deal. Don't fuck it now – we'll live with it. It's not for long. Please, as a friend, do it. You know I wouldn't ask like this if it didn't mean a hell of a lot for me.' Tears coursed down his cheeks.

I felt terrible. It was only for a few months, and I would still be producing an important film. I'd still get my fee and my percentage. It wouldn't be for long. 'OK, Syd, I'll do it. I don't want to speak to anyone for a bit. You tell them we'll all meet tomorrow for a production conference, here at ten.'

Sydney got up smiling, a different man, the colour back in his cheeks. It wasn't immediately obvious to me what a mistake I'd made. At that moment all I could think of was my need for a good stiff drink.

11

Open Secrets

H aving agreed to work on the film after all, it was not much fun to learn during the next few weeks that the production funding was seemingly subject to interminable delay. I never did learn the actual reasons for this but a much more interesting development was that we were finally planning to shoot a film. Contracts and other documents began to flow in a torrent. It was agreed that Jeff Stein and I should go to New York as soon as possible to locate and obtain old film-library material on The Who and we pencilled in our first shooting days for the third week in July.

It was strange to be arranging a trip to New York and Los Angeles with Jeff as my travelling companion, but I had the comfort of knowing he was at least as uneasy as I was. My opinion now is that everyone else's effort at peacemaking had made us ever more aware that we were combatants. I had Bill Curbishley, Sydney and Roger Daltrey constantly telling me that 'we could all work things out'. Equally I'm certain that Jeff was telling the truth when he said that Townshend had convinced him to work with me for the common good.

By the time we arrived at Los Angeles in mid-June, we had all become immersed in our jobs. Although my memories of the time we spent chasing down old Who footage are a bit of a blur, adversity during our short stay drew us together to a point where I at least trusted him, although I don't know if this was reciprocated. Our days were spent in a detective-like slog of finding and then evaluating possible leads to film material that was to form part of the skeleton of *The Kids Are Alright*. But we also had many opportunities to socialise and one can evaluate a companion more easily over dinner or drinks than in the more charged world of the office. One night we went to a Hollywood discotheque, an experience I'll never forget.

There were five of us: me, Jeff and his lady Robyn – an effervescent elfin-like creature – and two friends of theirs – a young man and his girl. We went to the entrance of the place, which shall remain nameless, but an enormous individual blocked our path. Pointing to a sign which warned that wearers of open-toed shoes would not be admitted, he said that the gentlemen could enter but the ladies could not. As two other young men were at that moment entering in open leather sandals, we started to complain loudly but quickly became quiet when the pair held hands and kissed each other on the cheek before going into the forbidden club.

Still, we contrived an excuse to gain entrance, based on the oldest chestnut known to the western world: 'We're making a film with –' in our case The Who '– and we're looking for a location for a special sequence featuring the boys.'

Immediately the rules were forgotten and we were ushered into an enormous, cavernous room where lights strobed and flashed, leaving large areas dark or shaded. In contrast, the dance floor was starkly lit and on it an all-male crowd – who looked like rejects from casting call for a Fellini nightmare movie – were paired in bizarre twosomes, gyrating wildly to the loudest disco music I'd ever heard. It was as if the Devil himself was helping with another set of big bass drums.

We were now well aware that this was a homosexual club but we were amazed at the size and sheer weirdness of this place. There were guys with moustaches and muscles dressed in leather. Others in shorts and singlets writhed with incredible sensuality, while two more in Brooks Brothers suits looked particularly out of place in a passionate embrace. In the land of narcissism, this appeared to me one more slide into the total mire of complete decadence.

As we discussed our reactions over a drink, Jeff reinforced my previous concern for Keith Moon. He repeated his fear that Keith was going downhill rapidly. He had collapsed off his drum kit at a recent concert and had to be revived by oxygen straight from the tank. During one of the more famous occasions, Keith had been totally unconscious and no amount of ministrations could revive him. Eventually, a member of the concert audience answered the question which our table of experts guessed came from Pete Townshend: 'Is there a drummer in the house who knows our tunes?' Unlikely as it may seem, such a young man came forward and played with the band for the entire performance, apparently acquitting himself rather well.

After a brief stay, we flew back to New York. On our first night I joined Jeff and Eddie Rothkowitz for drinks at a bar. Eddie was about 40 years old, had jet-black hair and dark, soulful eyes set in a handsome, bearded face atop a stocky powerful frame. He was clad, seemingly always, in blue jeans, sneakers, loose shirt with a scarf at the neck.

As always, the talk came round to the film. Eddie was initially very cordial and explained why it was essential for Jeff that he (Rothkowitz) should work on the film as its editor, since his close assistance was essential to the youthful director. Every effort I made to reply was treated purely as an inconvenient noise to be endured by Eddie, who could talk the hind legs off a donkey. In vain, I tried to explain to Eddie and Jeff that we didn't have enough money to hire Eddie, because his cost would be extra to the plan and I didn't believe The Who would come up with any extra funding. As his normal address was New York – where he worked as an editor on fairly worthy but not first-line work – he'd have to receive location living expenses, air fare, a car, accommodation and an appropriate salary. We would also have to quickly obtain clearances for him as another

American technician from the English film union and the Department of Labour in the British government.

Eddie became angry with me, as if I'd conspired to make these situations difficult for him. We'd all drunk way too much at this point, so at Jeff's persistent nudging I agreed that if the money and work permit situations could be straightened out I'd be pleased to step out of that area of the film, thus putting Eddie in as editor.

The tensions lessened noticeably and one of the guys suggested we party at a nearby apartment. I don't recall much about the place except that it was dark and smelled of incense, stale beer and urine. A cross-section of New York's artistic underbelly was in attendance: models gone to seed, road managers of rock groups that hadn't yet made it, or were on the downward slope to nowhere. Everyone who was no one was there.

A beery giant with a bushy beard slapped me on the back after he'd been told I was one of the makers of the new Who movie. 'That's really great, man. You tell Pete that I said hello.' I nodded. 'I met him once years ago, great guy.' He laughed at some private joke and turned to his petite, bleached-blonde girlfriend, who giggled in my direction. 'It must be really great making movies like that, man. I mean, great,' she said in a high, nasal Brooklyn voice.

'Yeah, it's great,' I answered. She only wanted a simple answer, I thought.

Meanwhile, the other boys and girls in the room were busily discovering each other's bodies on growing piles of their discarded clothing. Here I was at my first New York orgy and I didn't have a lady to call my own, which was even worse than not getting invited in the first place.

Small groups of people were going into a side room to snort cocaine and two or three joints were circulating in our room. I wasn't a drug user and this made me stand out like a pork chop at a bar mitzvah. The girl nearest to me had scraggy, unwashed hair and dirty fingernails, so when she tried passing me the joint I refused it, saying I was jet-lagged. Later, I admit to taking a couple of puffs, and I did inhale, but by then things were already way out of hand.

A guy had asked me what I was drinking and I'd asked for a Bloody Mary. I drank it and moments later I began to feel uncoordinated and disoriented. First and foremost, I became very horny, which in itself wasn't terribly unusual but the fact that I wanted to screw any of the dogs still available was. It was like a bad early Peter Fonda movie: the room was becoming psychedelic, expanding until it filled my universe then shrinking until it was too small to hold me. I tried to tell Jeff something was horribly wrong with me but the words simply wouldn't come out coherently; everyone seemed to be looking at me and laughing. I wanted to kill them. I'd become totally paranoid.

Then it was as if someone had turned on a strobe light, which made me see selectively – eyes bulging, hands, breasts and teeth, all in horrific detail. Next I climbed out on to the fire escape and talked about how I was going to fly down the six or seven levels to the ground. Someone pulled me back into the room, but I became very aggressive and rushed into the elevator, followed by Jeff and Eddie, who decided that, if they couldn't stop me, they would try to shepherd me to safety. Apparently, I walked about 60 blocks in all, stopping in Times Square to pick a fight with a gang of black youths who backed away from me, certain in the knowledge that this Brit was either crazy or high; otherwise, they could have swatted me like a fly.

Eventually, just before dawn I slowed down enough for my companions to convince me that a taxi back to my hotel was preferable to walking all those miles. I can clearly recall sitting in the back of that yellow cab and climbing out of myself into the sky, free of the confines of my own body. I looked down through the roof of the cab on to my body, which sat slumped and still between Jeff and Eddie, who were talking about getting me medical attention if I didn't improve soon. I suddenly thought that if I didn't get back into my body immediately I'd die, so with the ease of Mandrake I rejoined myself. The next day, apart from the room swaying a bit, I felt much better. My drink had been spiked and I had learned an important lesson: never take refreshment from a stranger. I have to thank Eddie and Jeff for looking after me that night. But for them it could have all gone horribly wrong.

20 JULY 1977

I woke up at 6am, fresh and eager. After all those months, we were finally about to start filming and our collective pulse rate shot up in anticipation. Nothing in ordinary business is like the high you get from immortalising your dreams on film. It's more exciting partly because it's so hard to achieve, and partly because, like sex, the anticipation is generally better than the event.

Looking out of my car on the verdant country landscape, I thought about our preparations. Was everything and everyone organised and ready? What last-minute problems would arise? Had we made sufficiently effective contingency plans? I believed so and watched with satisfaction as our first workers began to arrive at the film studios at 7.30. We were to shoot our first sequence in Shepperton's aging film complex, about 20 miles south-west of London.

Although the countryside was charming to the eye, the film studio appeared like a stain soiling the neighbourhood. Its capacious sound stages were rundown, the whitewash on their broad flanks peeling off to reveal forlorn attempts to hide its real face, like an old whore using too much make-up to cover her wrinkled face. We were using this decaying studio rather than the more salubrious Pinewood (where our offices were situated) because The Who were concluding the purchase of an interest in Shepperton to add to their burgeoning communication empire.

Parked by the studio were four or five huge trucks, a mobile sound vehicle and a luxurious coach, all belonging to the group's trucking and facilities company. I went into the workshop, where Bob Pridden, who was in charge of musical equipment, was making sure that the bulky sound systems were moved safely to the rehearsal stage.

I followed the equipment being manhandled by The

Who's road crew into the cavernous soundstage and tried to imagine what was going to happen. We'd loosely planned our first couple of days of filming as a 'shake-down period', so that the group and the film people could get to know each other.

None of us knew what would happen when the band actually got together to play as a group for the first time in about a year.

I was very worried about how Jeff would deal with filming his idols. Was he properly prepared? Could he handle the technical complexities of multi-camera setups as well as the giant egos of the band? Secretly, so that Jeff wouldn't be embarrassed, I'd planned the day's directions in case he hadn't. As a director with plenty of experience in such situations, I knew what to do if necessary, but I didn't want to belittle Jeff in front of everyone on day one. I had the feeling that he was out of his depth, a well-intentioned and bright young man who simply had to learn on the job because he'd never filmed anything of consequence before. I smiled at the irony of the situation and hoped I would be wrong. Objectively, I was certain that Jeff and our film were bound to have problems, maybe terminal problems.

The camera crews and soundmen started to set up in front of the raised stage and the enormous music sound systems were carefully stacked and tested. Bob Pridden seemed to come alive as the microphones were activated and the energy level of everyone seemed to mount as lunchtime approached. By 1pm, everything was ready and we adjourned for our meal in anticipation of the group's arrival at 2pm.

Precisely on schedule Townshend and Entwistle arrived in two separate cars, while simultaneously from above came the roar of a helicopter. Daltrey was flying the red machine. 'Look at the way he's landing it, the silly jerk!' said Entwistle as the chopper roared diagonally down through the trees, seemingly almost touching them. Our cameraman, Tom Harrison, was instantly keen to film this exciting arrival but only just managed to catch a glimpse as Daltrey landed, then walked to our camera position and said hello.

'Can you do another landing for us, Roger?' I asked, indicating that the cameras hadn't been ready for his dramatic entrance.

'No, I don't think so, Tony. I don't want our film to be anything like that Led Zeppelin movie. You know what I mean – bloody long Cadillacs crossing the bridge in America. How bloody flash can you get? I'm a working-class boy and a helicopter doesn't fit into my kind of scene. Can you imagine what our fans would think if I arrived in a bloody chopper!'

'What difference does it make what anybody thinks?' I asked him. 'That's how you really travel, so why not show it?'

But Roger was adamant about his working-class image and wouldn't be filmed arriving other than on foot.

On stage the three members of the group tentatively said hello and began to tune up. There was still no sign of Keith Moon, although by now it was almost an hour past the group's call time. It should be remembered that this could be simply because he'd overslept – or possibly because he'd started World War Three and even now was negotiating his way out of some stinking jail on the other side of the world. It should also be understood that if the latter were the case I'd bet Keith would still turn up in one piece as if the whole adventure was totally without danger. He was wonderful in dodgy situations; it was as if he was born to bullshit his way out of trouble. He was the master of mayhem – until the day it was all to catch up with him.

We called his hotel several times but by 3.30pm I was getting very worried as I'd heard from Keith's minder, Dougal, that Moon had been out on the town the night before, wenching and boozing. But just as I was about to press the panic button Keith arrived. Without a word of apology or explanation, he leaped from the back of his limousine and greeted us in the manner of raucous royalty, waving madly and calling to the camera, 'Hello, my people! Welcome to Moon's world of madness!' With that, he charged into the dark studio, shouting greetings to his bemused colleagues, and leaped on to his drum kit, clambering over it into his seat with a demonic grin on his strangely bloated yet childlike face. Almost instantly the group became a unified entity – this is The Who! Then the tuning-up stopped and the music began. Our cameras captured this moment and it was sheer magic.

The power of The Who in action exploded my senses. I was standing immediately in front of the stage and the sound waves almost knocked me backwards. Immense raw power was pouring into our cameras and sound equipment. It was one of the most exciting moments of my life. I turned to look at the crew stationed around the studio; they all had grins on their faces, a mixture of astonishment and pleasure. Some of the older guys in the unit surreptitiously passed cotton wool from hand to hand and could be seen stuffing it into their ears under the earphones they needed to hear directions.

Jeff stood behind one camera on the left side of the stage. As the group went into another song, I ran between the cameras, giving impromptu directions to the crew, when my eyes were drawn to the darkly lit back of the studio; facing the stage were a growing group of breathless young fans. Somehow the word had got out that The Who were back together and playing again. It was nearly miraculous how they had heard, especially as it was in an out-of-the-way film studio, and the fact that it was totally soundproofed did nothing to deter these die-hard fans.

As I arrived at Jeff's position, the last notes of the group's second song died away. Before I could pull him away, Bill Curbishley interceded. 'Can you believe it? They're playing together here for free and I could pack Wembley Stadium with them for a bloody fortune.'

'Yeah,' I said. 'Would you excuse me and Jeff for a moment? I just want to have a quiet word in the back room with him.'

'Sure,' Jeff said, beginning to walk with me towards the back room.

'Hang on a second, you two – I don't want you two having a row on day one!'

'We're not going to have a row, are we, Tony?' asked Jeff, smiling.

I stifled my reply and walked with him into the more private surroundings of the back room. Before he could back off, I asked him, 'What's going on, Jeff?'

'I didn't want to get into anything heavy right now,' he replied. 'Just let some film through the cameras and keep it simple so the boys can get used to them without any pressure.'

'Jeff, if you've got the bloody Who playing, you've got to film it properly. How do you know you'll get another chance?'

Jeff got up from his wooden chair and rounded on me angrily. 'Don't pressure me! I've got ideas how I want to do this!'

Before he could finish, Daltrey appeared between us. 'Boys, boys, cool it or I'll bash both your fucking heads together!'

Both Jeff and I turned to face him. 'Roger, this is something we've got to sort out ourselves,' I said.

'No, it isn't,' Roger responded, then continued in a manner to which I would become accustomed and would get thoroughly sick of. 'I don't want you two going at it, Tony, especially when what you're on about is mostly sour grapes. Now, if you two really want to go at it, I'll get you some boxing gloves and we'll all watch you two bash each other's brains in.' Then, before either of us could respond, he walked out.

'You see what you did, Klinger? You upset Roger!'

'Come off it, Stein! You do your job and no one will get upset!'

Jeff's face creased into a smile. 'Look, let's both of us work on the camera positions together, just until things settle down.'

Sydney now appeared from the doorway, where he'd apparently been standing unnoticed through most of the conversation. 'Come on, boys! They're ready to play some more and Tom's asking for someone to tell him what to do.' Tom Harrison was the lighting cameraman and as such was responsible for implementing the director's instructions, which in accordance with Jeff's approach as yet hadn't been too plentiful.

We walked back into the stage area, to be met by a wall of sound as the band played on. Tom Harrison called me to one side and shouted to me above the music, asking for more detailed direction. Working with more than one camera is a bit like figuring out multiple three-dimensional jigsaws – without planning, you are lost. For the next couple of hours, I stuck to my new assignment with tight-lipped determination.

This stabilised the volatile situation with the camera people, who now were free to concentrate on the work at hand. I so strongly disagreed with Jeff's approach that I couldn't bear to look at him; only the buzz I got from the music released my tension. The group played with joy and exuberance, gradually letting their hair down as they jammed a medley of old Beach Boy classics. Moon humorously attempted vocals, while Daltrey hammed at harmonising. Townshend cavorted around the stage doing the Chuck Berry duck walk, while Entwistle relentlessly kept the bass line going.

No one from the financial side remarked that thousands of feet of film, and consequently plenty of money, was being expended. My instinct born from hard-won experience screamed at me to do something immediately, but what?

Usually every angle lens and move of your cameras has to be carefully mapped out so that afterwards you can tie it together in the editing room. All Jeff seemed to want were static wide-angle shots of the band on stage – very boring and repetitive visually, and really hard to edit. As the group broke for a coffee, I walked over to Sydney. I told him what I felt was happening, that we were losing control and perhaps had already done so.

Sydney agreed but felt that it wasn't yet hopeless. Bill Curbishley had already said to him that I should keep myself ready to take over directing in the next couple of days. 'Be patient, Tony. Let him have enough rope and Stein's sure to hang himself.'

'Sydney,' I replied, 'the way we're going, the whole film could get abandoned. We're about to multiply our budget by four times if we carry on like this. I'm going to put everything in writing, then no one can say later than I didn't warn them. What's more, if you know what's good for your arse, you'll do the same.'

'Why don't you write your memo about this to me, privately and confidentially?' Sydney suggested. 'Then I can deal with Bill behind the scenes to sort it out. Don't make a big fuss now – we could all suffer if the band see us openly fighting.'

I took note of what Sydney said because at that moment it seemed to make sense. I wish now that I'd ranted and raved, screamed my fears and made a scene that the group couldn't miss or misunderstand. But the truth is less dramatic and heroic: I nodded my agreement and carried on with the filming.

Jeff was a consummate politician. When, during the next break, I voiced my fears to him about going over budget and schedule, he smiled and said, 'They'll give us the extra money later when we need it.' I called Sydney over so that someone else could hear this and Jeff more or less repeated the statement, adding, 'If the boys like what's in the dailies, it will be OK. Trust me, I know how they think.'

'Why don't we tell them what you want to do and let them decide?' I asked, but Jeff just smiled and walked towards the back room, where the group and some of the crew were drinking coffee. I held Sydney back. 'I'm going to write that memo, Sydney, but I've got a horrible feeling he's right.'

Imagine yourself in that charged atmosphere under hot lights with super-loud music pounding away and maybe you can visualise how difficult it was to think clearly. You could almost touch the tension and anxiety in the studio. I wanted to scream.

I stalked into the back room with Sydney, who walked over to Townshend. They chatted amiably for a moment, then Sydney said, 'You know, I met you guys a long time ago. I was involved with setting up a concert with you on a bill about 11 or 12 years ago...'

Before he could finish, Pete jumped on to the wooden bench he'd been sitting on and wielded his guitar in the air above Sydney's head. 'It was you!' he shouted as Sydney skittered away at speed. 'I knew it was you, the dreadful

Sydney Rose, the man who caused all the bloody trouble to start with!' Then he playfully chased Sydney out of the room accompanied by our laughter.

Roger ushered me to one side. 'Have you geezers sorted yourselves out yet?'

I thought about it for a moment. If I answered truthfully it would be labelled as more sour grapes; if I didn't there would be a period of some peace before the shit hit the fan. I opted for peace and keeping my word to Sydney. 'Well, I think we're getting a little bit more organised now. If you can make sure that your mate Keith gets here on time in the future we'll be all set.'

'Do you hear that, Keith? You've gotta be on time tomorrow or it's trouble.' Although Roger said it lightly, Keith's attitude was one of acquiescence, nodding as he walked back into the studio. 'I'll make sure he's here on time. I'm not waiting for him again like a bleedin' idiot.'

We walked back into the stage area and filmed until I dismissed the unit at our wrap time of 8pm. I wondered out loud to Sydney if you could construct a solid building on such a shaky foundation.

Going home, I found my shoulders had become stiff and uncomfortable, the kind of feeling you get from unreleased tension. No amount of thinking got me any closer to a solution. If I went for Jeff, I might succeed in curbing his power over the short term but it would result in more bitter in-fighting. If I did nothing, I was walking away from my responsibility. I decided to watch developments, but it was harder to hide my concerns when I got home. My wife saw through my attempts to conceal the anxiety building inside me.

'Do what's right,' she said. 'No one can blame you for that.' As simply as that she crystallised my actions on the rest of the film. I would do what I believed to be correct, honest and right, and bugger the consequences. I slept well that night.

THURSDAY, 21 JULY

For day two we again called the artists for 2pm, with an 11am start for the crew. Before this we had a viewing of the previous day's work. About seven of us shuffled into the messy, undecorated projection room, but nobody from The Who's personnel was present. It's very hard to judge uncut film of a group playing music you can't yet hear. The cutting-room staff hadn't time to synchronise the material, but viewing it was not very exciting. None of the cameras was mobile, all the lenses were wide and fixed, all filming the same scenes from almost the same positions and angles. It was as if the cameras were impotent.

The crew were in a row behind Jeff, Sydney and me. There was silence except for the occasional comments on technical details; otherwise the only sounds were the whir of the projector, Jeff's voice quietly choosing his favourite shots from the wide choice available, and the production assistant's pencil scratching on her pad.

I was deeply concerned about what I considered to be the

poor results of our first day's work, but waited until the screening was completed and Jeff, Sydney and I were left alone in the screening room. 'Well, that wasn't very exciting, guys,' Jeff said. 'But I tell you, it's gonna be fine. You know, that was only like a rehearsal day for them and us, and there are some good bits in there once we've edited it properly.'

As he paused, I jumped in. 'Jeff, we're wasting time and money. You've got to plan your work.'

This time, Jeff butted in. 'I've got today's work all mapped out, but I'm not happy with the camera guys you gave me. After today, they've got to go – they're no bloody good.'

This was news to me – they seemed very good. The camera crew were being blamed for the shots that they had been ordered to do!

Sydney jumped to the camera crew's defence. 'They are excellent technicians. How can you want to get rid of them just like that after one day?'

Jeff's smile was now looking a bit strained. 'You chose him [Tom], so you guys fire him. I just don't want him or his people around. C'mon, we've got to be at the studio in 30 minutes – I'll see you there.' He started for the door.

'I'll sack him if you like,' I called after him, 'but the next one's all yours.'

'Good,' he replied as he left the room. 'That's exactly what I want.'

Sydney said he didn't think it was fair to sack Tom, as he'd done his work professionally and well. He took a puff on his second cigar of the morning. 'But if he gets his way, he'll be choosing the whole crew.'

We pondered this for a while. 'At least,' I said, 'if he gets to choose the next lot of crew he can't complain about the results they get. We'll pay the camera crew off.'

Sydney looked at his watch and we realised we only had minutes to get to the film studio for the day's shooting at Shepperton. On arriving at the studios, I walked into the small, cramped room we were using for our temporary production office to find a lawyer's letter specifying my director's credit if I should be forced to take over directing the picture if Jeff Stein were dismissed. I realised I was being used to pressure Jeff and had no doubt that he'd be told my contract contained this clause. It could only serve to make matters worse between us.

By the time I'd finished dealing with the papers it was lunchtime, so we set off for the local pub restaurant that served the studio personnel and the village residents. We all arrived at precisely the same moment as Keith Moon's luxury limousine. Out he bounded, greeting us all with effusive embraces and gestures of eternal friendship – kisses on the cheek, bear hugs and reminders that today, not only was he on time, but he was more than an hour early. 'OK, chaps, how about a small libation... or two?'

We crowded into the empty bar and sat at the nearest table to the door. After we'd ordered a round of drinks, Keith decided to move the table because he felt it was too claustrophobic. He pushed but nothing happened, so he pushed harder. Still no movement, so he whispered something into the ear of his assistant Dougal, who left the pub while we continued drinking and chatting. Moments later Keith was surreptitiously handed a screwdriver. 'Excuse me,' he said politely and slipped under the table.

We giggled like a bunch of kids as Keith crawled around, unscrewing the fixed tables, tabletops and chairs before sliding back into his chair, a smile of satisfaction on his face. 'What say we drink up and leave this establishment? I think it's got a very shaky future!'

Later, that day we heard that all those tables and chairs had collapsed, but of course none of us knew anything about it. Happily, the only damage done was to a few bums falling to the floor and some beer slopping on to their suddenly prostrate forms.

By the time we got back to the stage, most of our equipment was in position for our first sequence of the day. We'd set up a manic arrival scene with Keith dressed as a fireman on the back of an antiquated fire tender that we'd hired. We would set off some sulphur bombs inside the studio, which Keith would ignore to play his drums in the gathering smoke. Keith thoroughly relished the prospect of some organised pyrotechnic mayhem and by 3pm we had everything ready to go.

I was pleased that Jeff agreed to use the cameras in a looser, more mobile manner. I don't like jumpy or flashy cine verité-style footage, close shots that truncate movement or reactions or disorienting camera motion, but there is a happy medium between no motion or mobility and too much. Good camera moves are those the viewer isn't aware of.

The rehearsals went well except for the fact that the ancient fire truck had a tendency to stall every five yards. Coordinating this reluctant red appliance, the ever-wild Moon (now suitably dressed as a member of the London Fire Brigade), several impatient cameramen and a special-effects man, who was positively thrilled at the prospect of making a great deal of smoke, was a wonderful bit of movie madness to be involved with.

On take one the truck sputtered around but was too fast for the master camera shot. The smoke had already been sent billowing from the stage so we had to wait while it cleared enough to start again. Take two was a technical screw-up with a camera jamming. As still more smoke wafted from the stage, it proved difficult to back the truck around the corner. Take three went well – until Keith got a fit of the giggles when he saw the now monumental clouds of smoke through which he was due to travel. By this time, the smoke was becoming an impenetrable brown wall and I think the sound of coughing from within it amused Keith.

Take four. The shout went up, 'Roll 'em!' I cued the smoke and Jeff shouted 'Action fire truck!' down the walkie-talkie. This time all went well. The truck trundled into view, Keith leaped from the tender shouting some amusing nonsense and disappeared into the wall of smoke, followed by the cameras. Other cameras inside picked up the action as Keith smashed into the studio. As he clambered on to the stage I could hear our long-range cameras complaining into their walkie-talkies, 'I can't see the fucker through the smoke. Is that him there or is it the second coming? Should I keep rolling? We could call it *A Foggy Day in London Town*.'

'I see I'm here by myself – first again as usual," quipped Keith as he climbed over his drum kit on to his stool, undid the top buttons of his tunic and picked up his drumsticks. This vision of Keith – bearded, grinning, his arms raised with the sticks like some offering to the gods in the swirling smoke – will stay with me always. Suddenly, he smashed the sticks down on to the drum kit, again and again, faster ever faster. A tempo became a rhythm then a frantic beating of release. This was Keith as he'd once been, the best rock drummer in the world. But then, like a tropical storm, it was gone. The explosive power and the majesty evaporated as Keith's years of self-abuse caught up with him and he sat there, a deflated husk of a man wondering where youth, vitality and talent had gone.

We all applauded as he finished but by then the smoke was choking us and making our eyes water. As the cameras cut, we all streamed out of the stage to wait for it to clear. We spent about 30 minutes outside, which we used to film the other members of the group arriving, just in case this version would improve on the previous day's. When our enforced exile was no longer necessary, we all trooped back into the stage.

Now we set up our cameras inside the recording engineer's booth and filmed the group listening to their previous day's music. Their dialogue was witty and sharp.

Most of the time when they were together their chat, on or off camera, was like witnessing a double ping-pong match of the highest order — bags of movement, smashes and spins, but of very little substance to anyone outside that narrow world. How many wild nights can be fun? How many groupies leave anything but a stale aftertaste? How much raucous laughter was for real?

The band talked of their Canadian tour when they'd been arrested. On that occasion Bill Curbishley called for some writing paper and a pen and started his letter, 'Dear Mum, well, here I am again, in the shit...' The boys fell about remembering a day that certainly couldn't have been fun at the time. Luckily, their arrest had been very short-lived, so the group's attention turned to the present and plans for the future.

It was soon obvious that any planning discussion led to instant disagreements between Roger and Pete. Roger wanted to tour, whereas Pete wanted to get back into the studio to record a new album. John seemed enormously bored by the discussion and Keith wanted to do something, anything rather than sit on his butt and mentally decompose. Finally, after a little prompting by us, they improvised a conversation.

'I hear things didn't go too well for you at the doctor's, Pete,' said Keith.

'I beg your pardon?' asked Townshend, cupping his ear.

'I hear you've got a problem hearing, the doctors told you today.'

'I didn't hear that,' Pete stated emphatically. 'No, I went

to the doctor's in Harley Street with Bill and they told us that if I carry on playing this loud rock music I'll be totally deaf soon.'

'So what happened?' asked Keith.

'Well, Bill asked the doc what he meant. Did he mean that this poor boy wouldn't be able to play any more? How would this poor boy be able to make a living? So I asked him how serious my hearing problem was becoming, and he said I should learn to lip read.'

Pete, Keith and Roger all laughed, but, as I knew this to be true and serious news, I detected an undercurrent of concern in their flippant manner. Here was England's rock guru being struck down with the worst affliction possible for a rock'n'roller and he was able to joke about it. Even if this was stage courage, it still seemed commendably brave to me. I never once heard Pete complain about this problem, nor did anyone else on the film. He might do a lot of things that aren't likeable, but you have to admire his guts.

The group got back on stage and once again launched into a medley of great rock songs, their own and other people's. The standard of playing was higher than on the previous day, but it was very noticeable that Keith became exhausted after only about half an hour's light playing. I turned to Jeff and whispered, 'We've got to do his section of film real quick, he's not gonna be around for long.'

'You're right. That's exactly what I've been thinking,' Jeff replied.

'How much cocaine is he using?' I asked.

'Hell, I don't know – a whole lot plus the three or four bottles of booze a day means he can't last long, man. I don't know how he can stand up, let alone play.'

'Look at some of the old material we've got and it's hard to believe it's the same guy.' The films and videos we'd collected showed Moon as a rapier-thin, super-energetic young kid with an unending passion for life, people and fun that seemed as if it was going to go on forever. The Keith Moon at Shepperton was a bloated travesty of that kid, a man with nowhere to go but up in smoke.

During the day, I made it plain to everyone that, if we continued in the same vein as we had started, we would completely destroy all previous schedules, budgets and cash-flow projections. Jeff reiterated his demands of 1 July – when he'd again phoned me collect from New York – for a bigger credit, a larger percentage and core money in fees. He also insisted on half his fee immediately, plus expenses and immediate work clearance from the UK government for him and his editor, Eddie Rothkowitz, in terms that were equally strident.

We'd argued loud and long. Jeff felt we were intentionally dragging our feet, though there was just no way anyone could pressurise the British government into giving speedy work permits, even to rock's finest. I also have to own up to a hearty dislike of Eddie Rothkowitz, which he'd compounded by telling me that without him I'd be making a home movie. He had said this at the same time as he and Jeff were asking for my help in getting him passed by the union so that they in turn would intercede with the government, who had already officially turned down his application.

One essential fact about people afflicted with terminal film disease – I'll call them filmaholics – is that we will lie, cheat, steal, mortgage our houses, our future, hock our cars, desert our women, anything to be involved with making the film which is our fix at that moment. Indicative of the risks we're prepared to take is the sure knowledge that more than 99 per cent of our dreams become burst bubbles, which leaves the average filmaholic less than one per cent of his time to make 100 per cent of his living.

Personally, I've set up productions on my American Express card when promised funds haven't materialised on some far-flung and inaccessible location. Jeff and I had gone to Los Angeles without money because Bill Curbishley had assured us that MCA, The Who's American record company at the time, would advance us about $16,000 when we arrived. This filmaholic disease has thankfully diminished within me to the extent that now I need less regular fixes and my romantic involvement with the medium is now tempered with the knowledge that I'm not making love to a pristine woman but am about to be fucked by a gigantic blowsy whore – which is fine if you know that sometimes you'll catch nasty diseases.

Filming continued throughout the afternoon and we all could forget our problems while watching the band power their way through their musical muscle-flexing. At 7pm we called it a day.

That night I went home to my study and sat down to compose a memorandum on my yellow legal pad, addressing it private and confidential to Sydney Rose. It detailed my deeply felt reservations about the problems looming for the production, both artistically and financially, if we continued in the same way we'd started. I also pointed out that I didn't feel I should comment artistically since I had been the alternate director and didn't want my opinions to be viewed in that jaundiced light.

At this stage, I was about to go to Los Angeles again to set up the Keith Moon shoot, while Jeff, Bill and Sydney went to New York to tie up the legalities on some of the library footage and hopefully locate more new material. But since the workings on the film had in my view deteriorated still further, I felt forced to send another more comprehensive memo to Sydney on the 29th. These memos, you'll remember, were private and confidential.

Unknown to me, Sydney then sent a copy of my first memo to Bill, with a cover letter emphasising the same points. A couple of days later Sydney telephoned me and described the following version of events, which I later managed to verify via the participants.

FRIDAY, 29 JULY, 9.45AM, A SUITE IN THE PLAZA HOTEL, NEW YORK

Sydney showed Bill my first memo and his cover letter. Bill agreed with the contents and sentiments they contained and telephoned me at my office in Pinewood Studios. We discussed the problems in detail and paid particular regard to the enormous projected cost overruns. After speaking with me, Bill phoned Jeff and arranged to see him that evening at 6pm.

At 6.45pm, Sydney arrived to see Bill, before the latter had to leave for London later that evening. Bill was still ensconced with Jeff so Sydney waited in another room. Eventually, Bill called Sydney in and told him that not only had he told Jeff about my memo and Sydney's letter, but he had also given him a copy. Jeff blew his stack.

'I don't know if this has been engineered so that Tony can direct,' Bill said. 'How about it, Sydney?

'No way,' Sydney replied.

Bill seemed happy with that and Sydney managed to smooth Jeff's ruffled feathers but he was sure that, when Jeff and I next met in Los Angeles, there would be big trouble. Jeff couldn't see any possible truth or merit in any of my reasoning.

The following day, Bill saw the Shepperton rushes in London and telephoned Jeff to tell him they were OK, causing Jeff to say, 'I don't know what all the fuss was about.' Sydney tried telling him and Bill that my memo's main concern was the budget, something reinforced by my second memo, which Sydney had just received.

Sydney felt Bill should not have told Jeff and broken his confidence and I felt the same way about my private memo being copied by Sydney and passed on to Bill. Once I'd accepted this intolerable situation, everything that flowed from it was partly my own fault. But I was a cocky bastard, certain that right conquers all and that it would only be a matter of time before The Who would see I was telling the truth and do what I wanted.

That same day, I left for Los Angeles. It was to be my last calm moment before the storm.

12

Shooting Keith Moon: Loony Tunes

It was one of those hot, dry days that even the ocean breeze does nothing to cool. We were in Malibu to film Keith Moon and gradually pandemonium was replacing organisation as our production's coin of the realm. We hadn't even started filming Keith and already schedules, budgets and ideas were being scrapped.

Even after shooting with Keith in Shepperton, I wasn't prepared for the chaos he caused us. I'd arrived in Los Angeles 15 days before shooting was due to start, so that I could engage staff, hire equipment and everything one normally needs. I'd done that kind of thing countless times without a hitch, but on those occasions I'd worked with real easy people, like the guys from Deep Purple or Lee Marvin, Roger Moore and Mickey Rooney. When Keith met us for a pre-production chat, I knew I'd have to forget everything I'd learned.

Jeff, Pete Nevard (the cameraman for this part of the shoot), Sydney and I arrived at Keith's house on the Malibu coast at 3pm, to be greeted by Dougal, Keith's man Friday, who apologetically told us that Moon was still asleep.

While we waited, we used the time to scout Keith's house. Our guide was his live-in girlfriend, Annette Walter Lax, an attractive, lithe, young blonde from Belgium, who was dressed in a translucent, short white nightie. It was the only clothing I ever saw her wear.

Later that afternoon, we met Keith and went to a local bar, where drinks were handed round. None of us was becoming drunk but I could detect the beginnings of an all-night session. I signalled to Dougal behind Keith's back and Dougal surreptitiously edged nearer to my bar stool.

'Can you get him to bed, Dougal?' I asked quietly.

'You fucking try,' he replied even more softly.

'We're filming first thing. You're his minder, get him to bed!' I whispered with more urgency as more rounds of drinks were consumed with bewildering speed.

'C'mon, Keith, it's time to hit the bricks. These guys will be filming you first thing. You wanna look good for the cameras, don't you?' Dougal implored.

'Yeah, Keith, we've all got to set up early,' I said, getting up.

Keith glared at us and ordered another brandy. I turned to Sydney and Jeff and asked for one of them to intercede with Keith.

'We really should be going now, Keith. It's nearly midnight,' said Sydney.

'If you want to go home now, you go home. I'm staying for some more to drink and maybe I'll fuck one or two of these young ladies while I'm at it!'

Sydney backed away a couple of steps. 'But we've booked the crew and equipment to be ready to start at your house at eight o'clock,' he answered quietly.

'You are here to make a documentary on me as I am, and that means you will document what I do, not what you want me to do. If that means me staying up all night and you not being able to film me 'cos I'm in bed in the morning, then you'll have to film me sleeping in my fucking bedroom, won't you!'

Sydney flinched visibly from the tongue-lashing, and we both tried calming Keith down. Eventually, Jeff Stein interjected, 'Hey, Keith, if that's what you want us to do that's what we'll do, but it's going to be real boring, lots of film of you sleeping.'

Keith sat down again and sipped his drink.

'But we've got a schedule and a budget, they'll get all screwed up,' added Sydney, instantly regretting the words as Keith jumped back up.

'Fuck your schedule!' He jabbed his finger into Sydney's chest. 'And fuck your budget, and fuck you!'

Sydney calmly held up his hand in the universal gesture of submission, but Keith was relentless. 'You're gonna learn what a week with Moon's all about!'

I tried to calm it down. 'Keith, if we go on like that, film you sleeping, starting late, screwing around for no reason, we'll be out of film stock on day one. We'll have a crew permanently charging us overtime. We'll run out of money and, as it's partly your money, we're only trying to look after your interests, otherwise you'll blow the budget to pieces.'

Keith was now angrier than ever and turned his venom on me. 'I just told him. Now I'll tell you. Fuck your budgets and schedules. If you need more money or stock or anything else, I'll get it for you!'

I could have walked out and left him to it, but I decided to pry him loose more patiently. I certainly couldn't leave the place without Keith. He might vanish for days and then we'd be up the creek without a paddle.

Another solid hour of boozing took place, with Keith enjoying it more each time one of us looked pointedly at our watch. At last he got fed up with the game and said he was ready to go home, but on the way to the door he spotted two young women. 'Hello, my dears. Care for a spin in the motor?' They giggled and nodded their heads.

Dougal leaned towards me and whispered, 'For fuck's sake, don't let him get behind the wheel. He's bloody death in motors. He'll get us all locked up!'

It was clear Dougal meant this because he tried to block the door, but Keith wasn't in the mood for truculent employees. 'Now give me the keys, dear boy. I hate to keep the ladies waiting for a spin in the Excalibur, you know.' Keith grabbed the keys from Dougal and dashed for the flashy white car. It was an extraordinary vehicle, very long in the style of a 1930s roadster with running boards on either side. It was convertible, with big chrome exhausts fanning out of its front and sweeping back for most of its length. I believe Liberace had owned it previously. All it needed was a candelabra on the bonnet; it already had the fur seats.

We chased after Keith but it was too late; he jumped behind the wheel and gunned the enormously powerful engine. 'He's not very good with gears or steering when he's sober,' Dougal called out, 'so watch yourself when he's pissed!'

Keith jammed the car into gear and headed directly into the oncoming traffic on the Pacific Coast Highway. Brakes squealed but somehow Keith managed to miss all the irate drivers screaming abuse at his rapidly disappearing tail lights. I could hardly bear to watch the mayhem, which suddenly increased as Keith executed a wild, wheel-spinning U-turn and roared back towards us at max speed. We scattered, but it was on us before we could reach safety, stopping with only inches to spare.

'I forgot you, dear boy,' Keith called calmly to Dougal. 'Come along, hop in.' As Dougal reluctantly obeyed, Keith turned to us. 'Nice motor, isn't it? See you chaps in the morning. Look after yourselves.'

As the roadster roared off into the night I turned to my colleagues and said, 'That guy's not going to live another year. If the drugs and booze don't get him, the driving will.'

Everyone agreed, and Jeff added, 'I'll only be happy when we've finished filming him this week. Who knows if he'll be around after that?' It was obvious to anyone who met Keith at this stage that he was staring imminent death directly in the eye, and laughing at it.

Monday, 8 August, Moon Shoot, Day 1

After collecting the cameras, lights and sound equipment from various film rental companies in Los Angeles, the crew dutifully arrived at Keith's house at 9.30am. Moon was as good as his word and was sound asleep in his bedroom. As Jeff and I entered the room to try to wake him, I looked around the gaudy, elaborately over-decorated room. Shaggy, pastel-shaded, deep-pile carpets clashed with flocked patterned wallpaper. The bed was a wooden four-poster with a huge canopy, which seemed odd and incongruous in a summery beach house.

Because Jeff thought he might want to film Keith in some of his strange costumes, we looked into Keith's clothes closet. It was as big as some people's bedrooms, about 18 feet long by 8 feet deep. There were rows and rows of shirts, hundreds of them, and similarly huge quantities of jackets, trousers, shoes and T-shirts made the huge closet feel small and claustrophobic. There were some good quality items – silk shirts, hand-tooled leather shoes – but most of the clothing was gaudy and strangely dated, as if Keith still yearned for the sartorially more liberated 1960s and early 1970s, when the Beau Brummel look was fashionable. 'I don't think he's ever thrown a thing out,' said Jeff. I nodded in agreement. It seemed as if Keith still had every piece of clothing that he'd ever worn.

We decided to set up the cameras and lights in the living room, which was on the middle floor of the wooden three-storey house, and took an early lunch.

I had engaged a young female production assistant to work on the Moon in Malibu shoot. I'll call her Missy to save her any embarrassment. She looked like a freshly scrubbed convent girl of about 20, wearing glasses and with black hair in neat braids topping out her carefully clothed, seemingly prim body. Missy had the education and job qualifications so I put her to work.

It was soon apparent that she had an uncontrollable crush on Moon. When she saw Keith for the first time, she turned to me and whispered, 'Is it OK for me to fuck him now?'

I was somewhat surprised: here was this respectable young lady writhing in excitement at the mere sight of Moon's face, which at 2.15pm was not a pretty sight. 'No,' I said. 'You can't fuck him now – he'll never get through the day if he started it that way. But I promise you that you can ball him as much as you like when we finish shooting this week.'

Thereafter, she was always asking me for the go ahead, like a puppy dog waiting for its master to throw the bone.

That evening she became particularly excited when we were filming a sequence that brought Keith together with a life-sized blow-up female doll. Missy suggested that she take the doll's place on the kitchen table. Keith overheard and was quite taken with the idea; I think it was the glasses that captivated him. Now I could put him in promise land too. 'Behave yourself, Keith, and you can have her when we've finished,' I said, to his obvious delight.

After groping the private parts of both the life-like doll

and the doll-like production assistant, Keith sat in his lounge ready to answer questions — or rather he challenged us to ask them.

Jeff and I had previously agreed to keep Moon bubbling by using an unusual interrogation technique. If Keith's answers became pat or boring, we would alternate the questioner. Jeff started the ball rolling, I prodded it on and Sydney also tried prying Keith loose for his prearranged party pieces.

Our first aim was to discover if The Who were ever going to get back together to make albums or tour, but, try as we might, he would only make jokes, about Roger's twirling mike being a means of shredding vegetables thrown by angry fans and enabling Keith to eat salad. His general comments on Daltrey were acid but amusing, as were those on the other band members.

Eventually, Pete Nevard, the cameraman, said 'C'mon, Keith, that's bullshit. Tell us the truth.'

Keith instantly became serious again. 'You want the truth? You can't afford the truth from me — I'm too expensive.'

Jeff asked him if the group would continue if anyone left. Moon said no one would leave. Jeff persisted. 'But if anyone did go would you replace him?' Keith adamantly refused to divulge anything about his inner self. I began to think there was none, that the man was a husk, a shell so filled with booze and drugs that there wasn't room for anything else. For his breakfast, which took place at 4pm in the morning room overlooking the beautiful beach, he drank a bottle of brandy, which had the effect of bringing him down from the giddy heights to which the afternoon's first line of cocaine had taken him.

For a while we talked almost coherently as we took the filming out on to the patio, but then Keith spotted two bikini-clad girls jogging past on the beach some 35 feet below. 'Hello, girls!' he shouted. 'Want to make it with a rock star?'

The girls ignored him and kept jogging.

'Snobs!' yelled Dougal.

'Why don't we take in the sea air, chaps?' asked Keith, leaping down the outside stairs two at a time in pursuit of the now-distant girls. A plane flew low overhead and Keith stopped running for a moment. 'Hello, there we go, lads, another Pearl Harbor!' And with that he strode off into the distance, followed by Dougal and Sydney.

Before the rest of us could get involved in the madcap chase, Jeff called me aside. 'It's a trap, Tony. If we set the camera up here on a zoom lens we should get some fun action on the beach.'

I didn't know what he meant, but, as Keith was now about 300 yards away with Sydney puffing a long way behind, I wasn't against standing where I was.

'Would you boys like something to drink?' asked Annette.

I followed her into the kitchen. She was a pleasure to follow, her centrefold body clad only in that almost transparent nightie. I took a white wine and wondered out loud, 'You must be a very strong lady to deal with Keith.'

She smiled. 'I'm no groupie, you know?' she said in her attractive accent. I knew her family was wealthy. 'I love him,' she carried on. 'I'd have to love him to stay with him. You know he can't do it any more.'

I understood her to mean that Keith was impotent, which I found hard to believe. 'You're joking! He's always chasing girls.' I regretted saying it as I saw the hurt flitter across her perfect face, but then she smiled.

'He can chase all he likes, Tony. He can't do anything when he catches them anyway.'

She brushed past me very sexily on the way out of the kitchen, and just as I was thinking, If only... I heard Jeff shout, 'Come and look at this, Tony!' from outside.

I rushed out on to the patio and saw Sydney in deep trouble at the ocean edge. Dougal had appeared from behind Sydney, grabbed him in a chokehold and dragged him backwards into the water. Sydney's nervous laugh changed to shouts for help as Keith took off his white silk scarf and wrapped it tightly around Sydney's collar. Now the rock star and his roadie forced the defenceless man under water and held him there. The joke was becoming a nightmare. As the seconds turned into a full minute and Keith didn't respond to our screams to stop, I rushed down to the beach, grabbing a pool cue on the way. By the time I got on to the sand, Keith and Dougal had relented and were leading the spluttering Sydney back to the shore, apologising profusely like kids after a harmless prank.

I saw that my friend was OK but still shaky, and one of the camera assistants led him inside to dry off. Keith walked towards me and I was sure that Dougal must be approaching me from the rear. 'You see, Tony, now Sydney and me, we're mates. We've had a bit of fun together.'

As he stepped closer to me I revealed the pool cue. 'You try that shit on me, Keith...' I turned and did indeed see Dougal approaching from behind.

Keith backed off and signalled Dougal to do likewise.

'Tony, don't take it all so bloody serious,' he said, smiling. 'It's only a bit of fun. We're all mates here, aren't we?'

'Sure we are, Keith,' I replied, also smiling, but I never turned my back on him again.

We returned to the house and I checked to see how Sydney was. I discovered the camera crew filming him as he meticulously and methodically laid out the soaking wet $6,000 cash he'd had in his pocket when he'd been dunked. Standing there in shorts, he began trying to blow-dry the money, which of course flew in every direction. It was a scene worthy of Chaplin.

Keith now telephoned Ringo Starr to see if he'd like to come over later in the week to take part in the filming. Simultaneously the doorbell rang and Missy let in a man who I learned was Rick Danko, who used to play with The Band. Danko was already bombed out of his skull. As he and Keith greeted each other, we decided to film the incredible array of gold and platinum discs that covered every wall.

'How many of these have you got?' Jeff asked. 'What do they mean to you?'

'Oh, those,' Keith said, waving airily at the walls. 'Those are just wall coverings. They're much cheaper than wallpaper. They mean a lot to me – if I didn't have them, I'd have to buy miles of bloody paper!'

With the arrival of Danko, the shooting degenerated. Keith

seemed hell-bent on becoming just as smashed as his guest, and they sat playing cards and talking nonsense. The boredom of watching two drunks perform card tricks that don't work is something I can recommend to all insomniacs. Eventually, we called a wrap at about 6pm. As the crew began clearing up the equipment, Sydney and I left for our hotel.

TUESDAY, 9 AUGUST, DAY 2

Since we'd finished slightly later than a normal day on Monday, we set a call time of 10.30 the next morning. This way I hoped to give Keith a chance of being up and ready when we were, but only Annette was awake. After telling us Keith was still sleeping, she said, 'You know we've had a complaint from our neighbours about filming on the beach yesterday. You'd better go and talk to them.'

'Sure,' I replied. 'Do you know them well?'

'Yeah,' said Jeff, 'it's Steve McQueen and Ali McGraw. He threatened to blow Keith's head off because Keith pushed his kid down the stairs.'

'When?' I asked, hoping it had been a few years ago but thinking, Shit, what next?

'Recently,' Annette replied. 'He's been upset with us since Keith dressed up as a Nazi SS officer and marched to their bedroom window at dawn and saluted them. Steve chased Keith away and told him that, if he came back, he'd tell his dogs to tear Keith's throat out.'

I'd heard McQueen was a tough character, but this sounded like Mission Impossible. 'OK, I'll go around and see what I can do, but if I'm not back in 30 minutes, come looking.'

I walked the 30 or 40 yards to the next house, past the empty lot McQueen also owned to ensure his privacy. Nervously, I rang the doorbell. I heard a dog bark, and visions of the Hound of the Baskervilles rushed through my mind.

The door opened and I saw Ali McGraw, a truly handsome woman, looking at me enquiringly. 'Can I help you?' she asked.

I said that I was the movie producer filming next door and I felt that I owed her and Mr McQueen an explanation and an apology.

'You'd better come in,' she said and led me to the breakfast room, which was so full of plants and flowers it felt like Kew Gardens. 'Would you like a coffee?'

'Yes please.'

She poured me some into a mug. 'I'll get Steve.' She went into another room and I heard a low growl behind me. Slowly I turned my head and there sat two very big, very hostile dogs. I think they were Doberman Pinschers, but I didn't stare at them in case it upset them.

McQueen entered the room. He looked distinctly unfriendly too. 'What are you filming?' he asked. 'I guess you've heard I'm not too happy with your friend next door. You tell him these dogs are killers. If him or you come on to my land they'll attack and it won't be anyone's fault but yours.' He said it quietly but with enough conviction to make me a believer.

'Mr McQueen, I'm sorry if we crossed on to your land yesterday, but I honestly did not know you owned it. It won't happen again. I'm sorry for the inconvenience, but I think all this stuff about killer dogs is a bit unnecessary.'

'Yeah, Steve, cut it out,' said Ali McGraw.

'We thought you might be trying to sneak shots of us,' McQueen said. 'What is it you're doing?

Looking at his bearded face, I recalled all the rumours I'd heard about his weighing 300lbs and going to seed, but he looked good to me. The beard and long hair did not improve him, but he still had the edge physically on almost any man I have ever seen.

'We're shooting a film about Keith's group, The Who. We'll not be pointing the camera in this direction again.'

'That's just fine. See that you don't.' He got up, smiled and we shook hands. He had a wonderful smile that truly seemed to light up the room. He turned to go, but stopped. 'Oh, and good luck with your movie. I appreciate your coming round to tell us what you're doing. Bye now.' He left and I was ushered to the front door by Ms McGraw.

As I walked back to Moon's house, I thought to myself that I too would want to kill a neighbour like Keith. Once I'd explained things, however, both McQueen and McGraw had been charming, and I'd been star-struck.

Eventually at 1.30pm, we decided to film Keith sleeping, as he'd told us to. Jeff climbed above him on the bed and called out, 'Keith Moon Shoot, Take 37!' and smashed the clapperboard shut. Keith surfaced like Moby Dick – from a great depth but fast – helped by yet more cocaine.

The day's filming was brightened only by Missy showing me, and anyone else who'd look, that she was wearing frilly black underwear, garter belts and fishnet stockings. Missy had a great arse, which she told me had been featured in a blue-tinged film. Apart from this delightful interlude, things were quiet and, after some more interviews had been shot, filming concluded at 7pm.

WEDNESDAY, 10 AUGUST, DAY 3

We decided to start filming even later this day and catch Keith at his peak in the twilight hours. We hired a giant Lincoln limousine and the intrepid film crew duly followed as Keith visited a couple of his favourite watering holes, The Crazy Horse Club and Alice's Restaurant, from both of which he gained female companionship. He threw the film people out of the Lincoln so he could have more room to fit in girls, but eventually he was content to have three in the back with him. He had one hand up a blonde's skirt, the other hand was massaging the second girl's breasts, while the third giggled and unzipped her trousers. The limo drove off as Keith buried his face in as much womanly flesh as his mouth could swallow.

We followed the limousine, which then led the film crew to a sexual-appliance shop called The Pleasure Chest. Keith led the way down to the dungeon, which contained a galaxy of sado-masochistic delights – whips, chains, leathers chastity belts and more. Keith had himself laced tightly into

121

a leather corset, to which he added black rubber underpants. His ensemble was completed by a black leather hood and mask with a zipper at the mouth. One of his female companions dressed in a more feminine version of the same thing without a mask. If you see the film I think you'll agree she looks better, her firm breasts and trim legs contrasting vividly with Keith's excess flab. 'OK, girl, get on with it,' he said to her.

'Do you think you're not regarded with proper seriousness by the rock'n'roll press?' asked Jeff as the young lady brought a leather whip down on to Keith's back.

'No, not at all,' he replied. 'Harder, darling, harder with the lashes,' he called to the bemused girl. 'Now back to your question – one sec, harder, girl!' He turned back to the camera: 'You can't get good help these days, can you?' The girl, who was uncertain whether to laugh, cry or simulate orgasm, whipped him harder. 'Not too hard, girl!' Keith called out.

The interview carried on in this style until about 2am when filming stopped. Keith wasn't through, however, and he vanished into the night with his companions and various implements, which we had to pay for. I can't imagine that too many other films have dildos, chains, whips and 'stay hard' creams on their cash-flow financial statements.

THURSDAY, 11 AUGUST, DAY 4

Keith had told us it was going to be his birthday shortly, so we'd arranged a party for him in Trancas, the restaurant and bar where we'd first met him. A big crowd of party guests, gatecrashers and the simply curious gathered as the last lights were put into position. By now, the whole crew had become a target for rock and film groupies. You couldn't move without getting women. I even had my bum pinched and began to feel indignant in much the same way I'm sure a girl does when the situations are reversed. I went up a couple of stairs to check if our surprise gift was ready for Keith and a truly Junoesque girl grabbed me in a bear hug and French kissed me, then said hello. It was an unusual experience to say the least and as it was only 9pm I could tell this might become an extremely interesting evening.

By about 10.30pm, the party was going full blast when Keith arrived like the Demon King. He was in a loon's heaven. I've never seen hands as fast as his grab so many bums or slip in so many cleavages, while still managing to keep irate boyfriends happy with calming words and soothing smiles. We wheeled in our giant birthday cake and Keith's eyes became like saucers as the top came off and out came our hired stripper, our cameras filming as she danced for him to his obvious delight.

Another cake, also big but this time real, was carried in. Keith looked at it then back at the undulating dancer. Suddenly, with a mighty roar he brought his hand down in a karate chop on to the cake, and the partygoers whooped in delight as he started to cover the dancer's body with cake. As she moved with increasing tempo, he smothered her breasts, buttocks, pubis and legs with the gooey mess, then started to lick it off her, taking them both to the floor in the process. Now her dance was that of passion. I don't think she was that good an actress.

As Keith's tongue darted between her legs and his hands rubbed and fondled her breasts, two or three other women disrobed and began to spread the cake on their own bodies. Keith was soon sandwiched in a melee of writhing limbs and taking off his clothes. Suddenly the club manager pulled me away. 'You gotta stop this right now,' he shouted above the loud music and encouraging crowd. 'I'll lose my goddam licence!'

'You try stopping him,' I shouted back.

'Well, get him into the john, at least,' he demanded. 'And I want your promise that you're going to pay for cleaning the carpets.'

'Sure we will,' I yelled back. 'If this doesn't work as a rock movie, we could make it in the porn market.'

I turned to see Keith trying to find more appendages to fill all the orifices that eager young women were shoving at him. Somehow we managed to get the whole group into the men's room. Being a rock star does have some things going for it, I thought as I left them to it, but the image of Keith in that tawdry toilet will remain etched in my mind forever. 'I'll fuck all five of you!' he was shouting, but it was the girls who were doing all the work. Keith was so fucked from so many wild nights that he didn't seem able to handle one woman, let alone five, although he was having a great time trying.

FRIDAY, 12 AUGUST, DAY 5

It had been arranged for Ringo Starr, an old friend of Keith, to appear in a cameo role that afternoon, the last day of the Moon shoot. They'd first become friendly when working together on a very good but underrated British film called *That'll be the Day*. Now Ringo was going to participate in loosening up his drinking companion and extract the truth from him for the cameras. I was looking forward to seeing the two great drumming lunatics in action together.

We had called our intrepid unit for 2pm at Keith's house. For the only time that week, he was ready for us. We dressed him as Long John Silver, complete with a rubber parrot perched on his shoulder, which he adored. His Robert Newton impression was excellent as he quoted poetry and doggerel on his golden beach. When he was acting Keith became a pleasure to be with. It was his only available release other than drumming, and he was naturally gifted at both.

A short while later, Ringo Starr arrived with his family. I'd never met the man before, although I had met all three other ex-Beatles, so I can't claim any familiarity. But Ringo was a smashing guy to work with – friendly, witty and full of good ideas. Of all the artists and performers I've encountered in the rock world, Ringo was the most polite, considerate and disciplined. He made our last day on Keith's beach a pleasure as he cajoled Keith into some gently humorous observations on the band and life in general.

'Is it true you threw a stick of dynamite down a hotel suite's toilet?'

'Yes I did, but it was only a small stick of dynamite.'

'Why did you throw a stick of dynamite down the toilet?'

'Well, if I held on to it I'd have blown my hand off.'

'But that doesn't answer the question. Why did you throw a stick of dynamite down the hotel's toilet?'

Moon looked left, so Ringo pointed his face to camera.

'The room needed airing and redecoration.'

'I see,' said the questioner. 'Did you drive a Rolls-Royce into a swimming pool and if so why?'

'To see if the bugger would float.'

'And did it?'

'No, it sank like a... Rolls-Royce.'

'And did you throw a TV set out of a Beverly Hills hotel on to the street below?'

'No, I never did.'

'Well, that's not what I heard.'

'I threw a TV set out of a New York hotel and rang down to room service to complain that my telly wasn't working. I threw a stereo system out of a Beverly Hills hotel.'

'Why was that?'

'I can't remember. To see if it bounced, I think.'

'And did it?'

'No, it fell to pieces. Jap rubbish.'

'Did you once flood a hotel in Holland?'

'No, only a bit of the hotel got flooded. I was trying to move a waterbed from one floor to another in the elevator and the doors closed on the bugger and it sort of sprung a leak. Most unfortunate.'

'Can I ask you why you were trying to move the

waterbed from floor to floor? Look at the camera when you answer, please – it's more sincere.'

'No, you may not ask.'

'I see. Do you have anything else you wish to tell your fans?'

'Yes. We're pissed.'

Ringo's hand covered his friend's mouth. 'He means we've been having to take too much medicine, boys and girls.'

This banter lasted for six or seven hours non-stop. We had more than an hour of it on film, although we ended up using only snatches of it.

Eventually, the shooting was wrapped and we had an informal party to celebrate its successful conclusion – or survival, depending on your point of view. I was standing with Keith and a couple of others when he saw some women on the beach. It was about midnight by then and Keith invited the girls up. They didn't reply, so, with brandy glass in hand, Keith leaped the 30-odd feet to the beach. Like rubber he bounced to the perpendicular with glass still in hand. 'He's like a cat with nine lives,' I said, to no one in particular.

'And he's had eight of them already,' responded someone else.

Missy appeared on the patio by my side. 'Now?' she asked.

'Yes,' I replied. 'Now's fine.'

About an hour later, I heard Jeff's voice calling my name from the middle distance. It took a while to track him down to a bathroom on the top deck, but, when I pushed the door open, it revealed a fabulously bizarre tableau. Keith was above Missy in the missionary position. She was partially clothed in frilly lace undergarments and a French maid's hairband and bib, and she didn't look prim now. Moon was fully dressed in his pirate's uniform except for his bum, which was naked and prominent.

Jeff was sitting on the closed lavatory and laughing himself silly, indicating to me that Keith couldn't get an erection and was therefore unable to penetrate Missy, who seemed lost in heaven being that close to ecstasy. As I watched, Keith leaned across her and opened a bathroom cabinet, pulling from it a varied collection of pornographic literature, which he placed over Missy's face in an effort at self-stimulation. Eventually, he found inspiration and to ecstatic groans of multi-orgasmic release Missy found her mate. Now I was certain: sex is mostly in the mind...

Before we left America, Sydney and I were telephoned by a New York representative of CBS Records, who asked us what company The Who would be signing with once they delivered the last album of their commitment to MCA Records. 'Whisper to Curbishley in his ear, we'll pay them 12 million dollars,' said this guy conspiratorially. Sydney and I looked at each other with our mouths open. At that time it was probably the highest record royalty advance guarantee ever offered.

'Tell him we're not authorised to get involved in making any deal. We're just making the film,' I said to Sydney, which he did.

Top and *Middle*: Tony Klinger and Roger Daltrey on the 'One of the Boys' video. It was directing Daltrey which led to *The Kids Are Alright*.

Bottom: Tony Klinger.

A performance on *Ready, Steady Go* in 1965.

John Entwistle.

John and Roger performing on TV.

Gathering around the Moon.

Above: The Who in 1965.

Below: Keith Moon, second from right, back row, on the set of *The Rock'n'Roll Circus*. The Who eventually obtained a clip of the film.

Above: The Who at the Isle of Wight Festival in 1969.

Below: Moon with former manager Kit Lambert in 1978.

Bill Curbishley and, left, his footballing brother Alan, at the launch of *Quadrophenia* and *Tommy* on DVD.

'Listen. you guys, if you get this deal done for us, we'll look after you real well. You understand me?' We understood him all right: a hefty bribe was being offered.

Afterwards, Sydney and I sat in his huge, rather tatty suite in the then wild Continental Hyatt House Hotel on Sunset Boulevard, then known as the Riot House. We'd become quiet, both lost in contemplation at this unsolicited offer. The first words out of our mouths showed me we weren't cut out for a life of shady dealing. 'We won't get any rewards for being straight, but I suppose we should tell Curbishley,' I said.

Sydney sighed. 'Of course, but let's just enjoy thinking about what we'd do with the money if we'd be a little less than honest. I'm just imagining where I'd put my pool and tennis court.'

As Sydney undid his tie and lay on the settee with hands clasped, dreaming wonderful dreams, I dialled Bill in London. After the normal pleasantries had been exchanged I told him about the CBS call.

'Whisper back to your pal, 14 million dollars,' was his reply.

'Listen, Bill, we're not your messengers. I'll give you his number and you can speak directly to him,' I said, effectively closing the door on Sydney and me receiving anything for setting this ball in motion. They never did make a deal, though: that honour eventually fell to another record label.

In a similar vein, Sydney and I had provisional discussions with several of the major US film distributors about our film, and two were interested enough to talk about making a blind bid in the region of $2,500,000 for the American distribution rights. These were unusual and tremendous offers, since all the companies had to go on was our chat and the fact that The Who and their music starred. The companies couldn't even see any film or even read a script. One of the more staid distributors asked me in exasperation how I'd describe the film.

Bluffing, I said, 'It's gonna be a cross between *Hellzapoppin'*, a classic Marx Brothers film and *Tommy*.'

The gent was as confused as ever, but doggedly pursued his quarry. 'So it's not a documentary really?' he asked.

'No, I wouldn't classify it as a documentary with all that implies. No, it's a funny, irreverent and exciting celebration of rock'n'roll. It's a unique film. It doesn't fit into any normal category.'

Sydney smiled slyly at my blarney.

'I'm still trying to get a handle on what this film's about,' the distributor continued. 'You know it's real important that we can work in concert. We've got the best distribution service and advertising department in the business. [Every distributor says this; some were a little less lousy than others.] But I do need to get a solid hold on the subject before we can brainstorm it out with the boys,' he concluded. This was one of the standard speeches so loved by all the American distribution houses. It meant nothing, but it did fill up some air.

I was having fun, however, so I decided to be the aggressor. 'Let me ask you, did you see *Easy Rider*?'

'Yes,' he answered, but I didn't like it much.'

'Did you understand it? I asked.

'No, not really. It didn't make any sense to me to be frank,' he responded.

'But even though you didn't understand it or like it, the film grossed something like 40 million dollars, didn't it? So what difference does it make if you like or understand our movie?'

It was a most unfair question, but the upshot was one of our offers in the millions which for a film that had no script, hadn't been shot, hadn't been properly funded and hadn't even had its library footage assembled wasn't too shabby an offer.

When we phoned Bill with the news, his response was typical. 'We'll get better than that later. Don't do any deals or make any commitment, OK?'

'But these offers are terrific, and they're only minimum guarantees,' Sydney protested. 'If the film performs well, then we'll get even more money. Who knows if they'll pay us this much, or anything, once they see the film? Say they don't like it, what then?'

'You've got to have more faith in the picture, you guys. This is just their first offer,' Bill said with finality.

'Bill,' I chipped in, 'there's no guarantees that later they'll do this kind of deal. It's a very good deal. Check it out by all means, but for God's sake don't let them go just like that. There's a time to negotiate a deal when it's hot and now feels like the time.'

Unfortunately, Bill wasn't willing to do any deal at that stage. Once again we'd been stymied and two big, rich companies that were hot to trot were told they would have to wait until we were good and ready. Never again were we able to stoke up the fires of their interest to the same intensity. The bird in the hand had flown.

13

War Is Declared

By late August, I was back in Pinewood Studios, as were all the other key production crew except for Jeff, who had stayed in California. Sydney began peppering him with requests for his detailed plans but there was no immediate response.

When Jeff returned to England, we seemed unable to make contact. Polite coolness was the order of the day, except that Jeff now became progressively more sarcastic to and about Sydney, which proved very embarrassing to everyone most of the time. I notified Jeff that all the industry and government ruling bodies had rejected our verbal and written appeals regarding his editor, Eddie Rothkowitz.

At this stage, Jeff hadn't worked with me or the other cutting-room staff at all. I'd roughly assembled some of the Shepperton material and had waited six and a half weeks for Jeff to see even these 35 minutes. After viewing less than ten minutes, his comment was: 'I wish you had waited until I'd seen this material in its original form, as pure rushes.'

Considering that this screening had taken one and a half months to come about, it didn't need a great imagination to see that our editing schedule was about to follow our other plans out the window. Jeff said that he wanted to meet up with the band's members on a one-to-one basis, as he thought this was the best method for making them give the extra funding the film was apparently going to need.

'Jeff,' I said, 'I'm not waiting around any more. I'm going to cut this picture, with you if you like, without you if you don't show up.'

By now you might have got the impression that I love to write memos and letters. That isn't the case. What I was doing was putting down for the record what I'd stated verbally face-to-face.

I had assumed that the band was intentionally holding money back from the production, which may or may not have been the case. Either way the results were the same: no money for anything on many occasions. Throughout the film's history, Sydney's company had received more bills than money to pay them. The only thing that kept the creditors at bay was the belief, shared by us all, that The Who had more than enough money to meet all their commitments to the film.

Pete Townshend's attitude to money and business was a revelation. He claimed in interviews of the period that he wasn't rich any more, because he'd invested in a lot of strange, diverse things that didn't do very well. His book-publishing company was doing very well, though. He'd got into very serious financial difficulties, really serious trouble, despite which he was still better off than most people. He described it as being richer than average.

He also admitted it was very tempting for The Who to stay together just for the money, because he thought they were near the end of their natural line as a unit in the early 1980s. He has publicly discussed how millions of pounds were blown on out-of-control business ventures, among other things. He also made the claim that, if they had known of the band's worsening finances, they could have helped bring their costs under control.

Jeff was going directly to him about the film, although we all had an agreement that all such discussions should go through Bill's office. This was making Bill and me progressively angrier, but no one seemed able to loosen the umbilical cord that ran between Townshend and Jeff. On each occasion, we saw members of the band at this stage, they told us – before we'd even had a chance to say hello – they didn't want to discuss the business side of the film.

15 SEPTEMBER 1977

The prevailing attitude on the film became even more discouraging. I confronted Jeff with Sydney present, and asked him, 'Did you see Pete about getting Eddie Rothkowitz on the picture?'

'Yes,' he replied, 'and he's given his go-ahead and so have the rest of the band, and so has Bill.'

I reminded him that all production matters were supposed to go through the production office and anything concerning the band via Bill, and that we'd made a deal to do it this way. 'Look, Jeff, you know we've got to work together or we'll all be in trouble. All we've asked for is some idea of what you want to do and how you want to do it. It's no secret that we're going over-budget, but now's the time to organise the film.'

Jeff replied, 'I told you before. I'm getting all the shoots worked out, and when I'm done I'll give it to you guys. What are you so worried about?'

Although we'd achieved nothing of substance, Sydney and I felt good: we had said what we felt. We telephoned Bill and told him about the meeting. Bill, clearly angry, said that enough was enough. 'Put it in writing to me, Tony, and I'll show it to the boys.'

I wrote the required letter to Bill, making the following point, 'No one wants this to be a really good film more than Sydney or I. I just wish they [the band] could understand that we're not breadheads – we really care.'

At this stage, the all-round pressures increased. I wrote a comprehensive letter to Sydney underlining all my fears. It was apparent to everyone on the production that the simmering conflicts which had been below the surface had now boiled over into open war. Our worst fears were realised: the film's crew was divided and spent more time scoring points with cheap shots than they did doing their jobs. Sydney and I visited Rock Films' lawyers at their invitation and we received a soothing pep talk, much sympathy, but no solutions.

The next day Jeff broke his writing embargo by sending us two memos. In one of them, he stated an absolute truth: 'We are all aware that most of our plans go out of the window with the daily changes of The Who's schedule which, of course, must dictate our own.' Jeff finished by stating that Bill was about to have a meeting with the band to discuss our future shooting plans and, after this meeting, which was to take place without any of the production people present, Jeff would be able to answer all our questions.

To put our ostracism from The Who in context I will compare our treatment to when I'd worked with other bands. Of comparable stature to The Who in importance and revenue were Deep Purple. While I worked with them, I had many meetings, both social and business, with Roger Glover, Jon Lord, Ian Paice and Ian Gillan. We had dinners together and chatted over drinks. I had been to some of their homes and they to mine. Although they had their fair share of lawyers, accountants and management, they never used them as an excuse or shield. If the Deep Purple guys had something to say to me, good or bad, they invariably said it to my face.

27 SEPTEMBER 1977

Sydney and I arrived at Bill's West End Office the next day at 11am. It soon became clear that Bill was looking for ways to ensure the film's success. We then raised a question that Sydney and I had often discussed in private.

'What's Jeff's influence with the band?' asked Sydney.

'Pete trusts him. He thinks Jeff will come through for the

film,' Bill answered. If anyone's got any ideas about how to keep the film on track, I'd be pleased to hear them. You tell me what you want.'

I told Sydney and Bill that I was determined to do everything in my power to work well with everyone on the picture for the greater good. 'Perhaps,' I said in an effort to convince myself as much as my listeners, 'if Jeff and I can work our problems out, the whole thing will start to improve.'

Bill applauded this attitude, and told us that extra funding would be approved once we'd got the figures broken down into our weekly cash-flow projections. We finished up on this note, and Sydney and I drove back to Pinewood Studios to catch up with our paperwork relating to the acquisition of library material on The Who.

You should understand the scope of this task. It involved tracking film clips in England, America, Holland, France, Belgium, Australia, Germany and Canada, plus many other less interesting sources. These countries each had multiple broadcasts on the band, which had usually originated in those countries when the band had toured them. Most, if not all, the countries had many broadcasting stations and no one knew which of them possessed the original tapes. Only the Germans, with typical and commendable efficiency, knew exactly what we were talking about. They tracked down all the many tapes they had on the band within one day and were ready, willing and able to negotiate an immediate deal.

The French, on the other hand, treated our repeated long-distance calls with Gallic indifference. The first three times we managed to get through to the state-controlled network, we were put on hold, although the operator was well aware we were calling from overseas. After narrowing down our richest sources of material to Hamburg and Paris, we decided to set off in pursuit of our film.

14

Fast Trips, Slow Women And Rude Frogs

10 OCTOBER 1977, HAMBURG, WEST GERMANY

When Jeff, Robyn (his lady friend) and I arrived at Hamburg airport, we almost stepped right back on the jet. When the door opened, we looked out to see a light tank with its cannon pointed right at us, ringed by soldiers sternly gazing in our direction. This impressive show of force was due to the recent activities of terrorist organisations in Germany, both domestic and imported. After descending gingerly to the cold, damp runway apron, we were ushered quickly to our hotel.

The cool, polite efficiency of Studio Hamburg, which is a part of the mighty PolyGram group, was an awesome delight. We'd mentally set aside three or four days to find the 20 film clips we believed they had somewhere in their vaults. Then, we had surmised, it would take at least the rest of the week to negotiate a deal for this very important source of material. Unbelievably, compared to the

141

protracted nature of our dealings with the English networks, the messy and complex American machinations or, even worse, the French stonewall, the Studio Hamburg people had every one of the 20 pieces of film ready for us on a viewing machine and neatly labelled.

Some of it we'd already obtained from a different source, but the old stuff was priceless, the *Tommy* material well shot, and the interviews unintentionally very funny. Imagine a very intellectual German interviewer confronting a progressively more bemused Townshend with questions like: 'Was it your intention to polarise and encapsulate the differing strains of socio-economic stratas within English society vis a vis the lack of senses in your vivid, impressionistic characterisation of Tommy?'

Townshend looked down at his nails during this startling and obscure attack of verbal diarrhoea. When it finally ended, Pete looked his man straight in the eye and eloquently replied, 'Yeah.' Adding a nice touch to all this nonsense were the German subtitles at the bottom of the screen. Jeff and I fell about laughing watching this and other similar faux pas, while the German technician who was running the viewing machine looked on stony-faced.

My notes on the trip make this point: 'The atmosphere on the movie, especially between me and Jeff, has suddenly and unexpectedly improved. Everyone is much happier, even friendly; calm before the storm?'

There had been a quantum leap in camaraderie between us. I think it might have been due to the very pleasant personality and calming influence of Robyn. We actually all seemed to be enjoying each other's company and having fun.

In hindsight, I think we were drawn together by leaving the film's base of operations, which had become a pressure cooker for us. Here, there was no one to observe and interpret our every action and consequent reaction. After 16 weeks of unending hostility, the calm was a blessed relief.

After viewing the film clips, we decided to try to obtain an option to acquire the total footage. Fearing our luck was now sure to run out, I entered the company executive's spartan offices and miraculously agreed a deal within 40 minutes. It was an amazingly satisfying experience, which unfortunately was not to be repeated elsewhere. After saying our goodbyes we were able to leave for Paris the same day.

10 OCTOBER 1977, PARIS, FRANCE

We disembarked at the futuristic but curiously soulless Charles de Gaulle airport and underwent the usual insane Parisian taxi ride to our hotel, which turned out to be a characterless counterpart to the airport. After checking in, I started making telephone calls to the stations from whom we had arranged to obtain viewings. No one was readily available, and the secretaries who took my calls were unanimously unhelpful. We decided to go and eat, and set off to a charming, old-fashioned restaurant.

After eating, our merry little group returned to the hotel. We had chosen it so that we could chase up The

Rolling Stones who were also staying there. Years previously they had commissioned a film called the *Rolling Stones Rock'n'roll Circus*, which had included a tremendous Who sequence. For reasons known only to themselves, the Stones had decided not to release their movie and were apparently not keen on allowing anyone else to take a section out of it. We were trying by every device we could think of to convince Mick Jagger, the Stones' top decision maker, to let us have this vital material. To this end Pete Townshend had handwritten a note that read:

6 October
Dear Mick,
After our phone call you OK'd Jeff Stein viewing the footage from the 'Circus' programme — he thinks it's great; as a result we would like to get a print for our rough cut. We could work out finance later if you wish. I really must thank you for your help. Much love to you and the guys in the band.
Love, Pete

We couldn't get directly to Mick so instead we handed the letter to Ian Stewart, who was the band's pianist and sixth member. It struck me how similar the Stones' entourage were to The Who's bunch of followers — so serious, pretentious and self-important, as if hidden in those guitars was the Holy Grail. It's even more galling when you want something from such a tightly knit, introverted organisation. Usually when you get to the star himself, you find he is less self-important and obnoxious than the guy

144

who delivers the tea. That guy is insecure because his hold on the high-paying gofer job is even more tenuous than most stars' position in the fickle world of rock stardom.

However, the end result was that we did obtain this excellent clip of The Who's performance from the Stones' film.

The following night, Jeff insisted we go to the Crazy Horse Club because he wanted ideas for the film's finale. I'll own up and say that I thought this link tenuous at best, but I wanted to see the famous Parisian nightspot in any event as it sounded like a fun plan. Although the club was very tourist-oriented, it was still a great evening and the show was head, shoulders and boobs above the usual dross one sees at an erotic presentation.

Our table was near the stage, with Japanese matrons hemming us in on our right and a bizarre group of assorted Taiwanese pensioners on our left. They clucked appreciatively when the uniformly gorgeous nude chorus line appeared on stage. It's difficult to think of filming when a bunch of beautiful, naked dancers are undulating an arm's length in front of you. The staging cleverly used lights to great advantage since the set was stark, angular and almost bare. As our currency vanished by the minute, I concluded that some locations were better to work in than others.

The next week was spent in pursuit of the elusive management figures of French television, which had just undergone a total, government-ordered reorganisation. Its former monolithic structure had been fragmented into several mutually competitive companies, thus complicating an already complex and confusing situation.

After much chasing around, we managed to at least verify the dates and places of the material we were looking for. To do this we had to examine, with a magnifying glass, several thousand stills and contact sheets that had been shot during The Who's various French appearances. Having identified the shots taken in television studios, we then whittled those photos down to a narrower group in which one could identify the TV studio's name on the side of the video cameras. We then crosschecked the dates with the photojournalists who had taken them. It was wonderful to be able to tell the Institute National Audio Visual, the clearing house for all such matters, that their repeated claims that no such films had ever been shot was bullshit!

Even so, this didn't seem to have any impact on the people at the Institute, who were either unwilling or unable to negotiate anything, even if by some chance they might locate the clips. They wouldn't even meet us to discuss it until they had had a few weeks to think about it. Despite their intransigence, I insisted on at least telling them the kind of deal we would like to do on the five clips they possessed somewhere within their labyrinthine organisation.

Less difficult to deal with was Radio Television Luxembourg via their office in Paris. This material had mostly been shot in the late 1960s, but unfortunately the company was of the opinion that these programmes had been broadcast live and direct from their studio, and were neither taped nor filmed. We then located, via RTL, a gentleman called Philippe Viaro who had directed the filming on a Who concert that RTL had mounted in Paris.

Sadly, the one and one half hours of this material that we saw was exclusively of the huge crowds waiting to enter the stadium and following them in while they watched the concert. This we certainly didn't need, since we already possessed footage from 28 cities and concerts with more than two million people watching The Who. Philippe explained that no filming had been allowed on the performance since the band had just concluded their deal for the film *Tommy* with Robert Stigwood, which precluded any filming of the band for one calendar year. I have no idea if this was correct, but it was sad to see the tired and hapless Philippe take his films on crowds out into the Paris night.

While in Paris, we also contacted other European TV companies in Sweden, Denmark and Holland, and managed to scrounge some clips from them without undue complication. So our European trip was justified by the acquisition of more than two and a half hours of original Who material that would give *The Kids Are Alright* a continental flavour, which we thought was needed to counterbalance our abundance of Anglo-Saxon material from England, America, Australia and Canada.

Gratefully, we packed our bags and left Paris, relieved to know we wouldn't have to spend any more time in the place. It would be the greatest city in the world but for its inhabitants.

15

True Situations

Soon after our return to England, Sydney joined us. He had been in the US, undertaking the Herculean task of chasing down American library footage. He was negotiating with 29 separate sources spread throughout the country and had somehow managed to bring a sense of order to that mountain of material.

Sydney asked me if I'd signed the non-disclosure letter yet. This was a letter that stated that I wouldn't disclose any information whatsoever relating to The Who or the band's individual members at any time prior to general release of the film to any person other than, in confidence, my professional advisers and union officials. I told Sydney for the second or third time that I'd never sign it. Sydney said that, although he agreed with me morally, he was going to sign it, just for a peaceful life.

Meanwhile, I'd also been diligently pursuing Eddie

Rothkowitz's work-permit situation. On 27 October, I had lunch with a union official to try to get their blessing for his employment on our production. Finally, they agreed to allow him in if we also employed a recognised British editor to 'double up' and paid this unnecessary extra man a proper weekly rate. This editor would have to actually work on the film; no phantom editor would be permitted. This meant we couldn't pay someone a nominal sum to stay home. The union also demanded that their man should get at least a co-editor credit on the film, and required me to be present in the cutting room if at all possible, so there would be at least two union-recognised, British editors on the film.

Although this would mean still more costs to the film, I provisionally agreed to do the deal wanted since the union weren't about to bend any further. It was essential to get our cutting room in action and, if getting Eddie in was the only solution that could work, I'd do it.

After lunch, I went to meet with Bill Curbishley and told him what had happened. He told me that I might have been wasting my time and showed me a letter he'd written to Pete Townshend and circulated to the band. In it he gave his forthright opinion on the progress of the film.

Curbishley told me that, whatever the band might think of Sydney and myself, we were efficient, honest, hardworking and creative. Bill also confirmed that we had earlier reached a verbal agreement for us to only contact individual members via him, and that Jeff had consistently chosen to deal directly with the band, including his most recent last visit to Pete.

The letter ended by asking the band for their total support in whatever measure he saw fit. He asked for it with some force and, it appeared to me, assurance borne of having had the band's tacit approval.

After this meeting, I spoke with Jeff by telephone and told him the bones of this letter to the band, and that Bill had informed me he would be showing it to Jeff. He told me all he'd ever wanted to do was obtain the deal he had originally been offered. I suggested to Jeff that not only were we dealing with a pragmatic problem, but also he had to face the fact that the only possible solution I could see him reaching would be to stick with his fees and percentage, etc., but to obtain remuneration on a pro rata basis for the additional weeks he would be working, to which he seemed amenable. It was the same thing I'd been saying for the past four months and I genuinely hoped that this would be the deal they'd reach. Otherwise, by the terms of my contract, I'd be lumbered with an impossible situation. If Jeff and Bill did agree along those lines, it would also assure us recompense for our extra efforts on The Who's behalf. Who said I wasn't Machiavellian?

This wasn't everything of substance that occurred during my meeting with Bill, but it does summarise the Jeff Stein situation fairly well. It had been in the spirit of our recently found friendship and obvious common interests that I'd immediately called Jeff and warned him of Bill's impending action. I had come to realise that Jeff's cause did have some justice in relation to his deal. My warning was a genuine effort on my part to build bridges and make peace:

I'd never have done so earlier – or later, in the light of events to come.

During our meeting, Bill had also telephoned the record company in Germany to draw down sufficient funds to cover The Who's various acquisitions and projects, including our film. Even more intriguing, I heard him discussing advance payment being made for a soundtrack album from 'the film currently being made'. This could only be our film. Remember, Bill had sworn to me before a room full of lawyers that there would never be a soundtrack album to silence my request to negotiate a percentage for the production executives, including myself. I also recalled that Bill had gone on to say that, if for some strange reason there was eventually an album, then he would negotiate our percentage participation in good faith at that time. I immediately reminded Bill of our understanding.

'I don't remember that at all, Tony. Are you sure I said that?' he asked me like a true innocent.

I won't go into the details here but let's say we never did agree this point. And so it came to pass that I came to believe I could no longer rely on his judgement or word as far as it concerned me. Once I had this firmly set in my mind, everything that flowed from our strange relationship made a kind of sense. Nobody's word on the film seemed to count for anything, and any time two or more of the senior personnel got chummy, somebody else would come along to split them up for some imagined advantage.

I had been commissioned to start writing a screenplay for a proposed Ken Russell picture called *Rock On* as soon as my contractual first call period on *The Kids* was over on 12 December, and by early November my eagerness to depart was at fever pitch. I'm not saying that I was glad to throw in the towel at the earliest opportunity, but I was looking forward to a new challenge unencumbered by the hostility and political intrigue on my current venture.

It's interesting to contrast the almost perfect working conditions our financiers, The Who, surrounded themselves in with the anarchy our film was from its inception. Bill made some telling points that I feel are fair commentary on the way the band see themselves. 'Do you know no one ever lost money working with the band? This is the best thing that's ever happened to you, Klinger. Why do you keep complaining?'

I ruminated for only a moment before answering. 'Bill, I had a nice house and good cars with a lovely family before I ever met you guys. I'll still have them when you're gone. You're not doing me any favours. You're paying me what you agreed to pay for a job you asked me to do. I'm not a poor relation. Why do you keep telling me that I should be grateful?'

Bill wasn't about to let it go at that. 'I don't see why you and Sydney should get any piece of the record royalties; they aren't your songs or your singing. Why do you think you should get a piece of the band's action? It's beyond me!'

'If we followed your argument to its logical conclusion, then the band shouldn't get any piece of the production end of the profits because they've got nothing to do with the creation of this film other than money,' I countered. 'But they still want, and get, the financier's shares and most of the producer's share. And I wouldn't be too surprised if they don't end up putting deferred fees down on the budget for themselves before those shares of profit even get to the calculator. I want you to understand I've worked on films that cost ten, twenty times more than this one. They didn't have a tenth as much aggravation and I don't think you're doing me any favours.'

I ached to say more, much more, but I knew none of it would make any difference. Despite my grave misgivings, I had to stick the film out till the end of my contract. Walking away was not something I could do. The film industry regards walking away from a contractual commitment as the ultimate betrayal. You just don't do it unless there is no other avenue open to you.

Although some of the anecdotes are amusing and other parts may seem glamorous, we were all being seriously damaged. Working this way was no day at the beach. I remember a young assistant agent, I think at Jack Gilardi's office at ICM, talking to me about a spoof project his clients were planning to produce about this time. His name was Dan Petrie Junior and this little film was called *This is Spinal Tap*. I think it's a great film and I am confident that Dan and his team knew exactly how close to reality their send-up really is.

During October and November, most of our time was spent pulling in and collating yet more library material from around the world. The extra footage included more than 50 pieces of film from various countries. Also, on 22

November we finally received a work permit clearance for Eddie Rothkowitz, although our funding for the extra expense hadn't yet come through.

Although physically still on the production, my heart was no longer in it. At home my wife received a phone call threatening her and our children's lives. I tried to calm her down, but she was disturbed beyond normal reasoning. The man, whose voice she hadn't recognised, had said, 'Get your old man to behave or we have you and your kids!' then hung up.

Immediately I contacted Sydney and Jeff, telling them of the obnoxious and cowardly call. Sydney commiserated, but Jeff reminded me that his London apartment had recently been broken into and ransacked. Most of his film research papers and personal accounts had been stolen, although other more immediately valuable items were left undisturbed. Finally and most worrying, the unknown intruders had left a razor-sharp breadknife plunged in his front door. We told Bill about these threatening occurrences, but he seemed to think they were the product of our over-active imaginations.

Nothing further occurred for several weeks, until I received a phone call from my bank, asking if my wife had authorised a young man to cash one of her cheques. I told them to keep the young man waiting while I called my wife to check it out. She told me she had no knowledge of any such cheque, which I told the bank, and they then told me the young man had just run out of their building.

I didn't have long to ponder before the telephone rang

again. It was my wife and she was nearly hysterical. 'Someone's just called me and he says he's coming to kill me! Please, Tony, come home quickly – I'm scared!'

'Lock all the doors and call the police,' I shouted. 'I'm coming home!' I slammed the phone down and told my secretary to get the police to my home quickly. I told her and Sydney what I'd just heard and got Sydney to drive me home. It was one of the worst 20 minutes of my life, but as ever Sydney was good news in a crisis: solid, old fashioned and trying to do the right thing.

A procession of nightmarish scenarios flashed through my mind as Sydney powered his little Italian roadster through the winding country lanes. We arrived at my house and gratefully saw there was a police car outside it. We rushed inside and found my wife safely being interviewed by a young police constable. 'Are you all right?' I asked.

'Yes,' she replied, 'but he just called again, just before the police officer arrived, and he said he's coming to kill me.'

The policeman finished taking her statement and said that now I was home he'd go have a look around our small country village to see if he could see anyone behaving strangely. But he'd keep close and be back later.

Shortly after he left, the phone rang again. This time I picked it up. A husky young man's voice, obviously in distress or under great strain, whispered, 'I'm here now to kill you.'

'Good, you slimy bastard, because I'm here waiting for you!' I answered. There was a pause as the caller realised my wife was no longer alone. 'Where are you, filth?' I demanded. 'I'm coming to get you!'

Caught off guard and apparently confused, he said, 'I'm in the phone box at the railway station. But you won't get here in time – I'll be gone.'

He hung up and I called the police, who had a man there within one minute. They found the phone booth empty, but discovered some empty pill bottles on the floor. Within an hour, they called again and told us they had arrested a young man who'd been walking on the railway line between Radlett and St Albans, drugged out of his skull and hoping to be run over by a train. Miraculously none had ridden those rails and the young man was presently under guard at the local hospital, having his stomach pumped. The policeman described him as about 20 years old, five feet nine inches tall, medium build, with carrot-red hair but bushy black eyebrows.

My wife, who was listening on the other line, instantly remembered the odd-job man we'd been using, who had dyed red hair. She gave the policeman his name, which the constable was able to corroborate. He was bound and arrested, and we discovered that he had stolen some cash from us and had a history of mental disorder. We didn't press charges. But we never did find out who had raided Jeff's apartment or threatened my kids by telephone.

More than ever, I now wanted to put distance between myself and this film. Too much turbulence and rubbish seemed to float in its orbit. I was deeply upset and frustrated by the possibility that someone I was working with had decided to attack my family and myself. If my worst suspicions were right, then this unknown co-worker was sicker and more evil than the disturbed odd-job man. At least his motives were fairly obvious and even understandable, but someone who sticks knives in doors and threatens women and children is truly sick, cowardly and beneath contempt.

Without direct evidence, I couldn't draw a connection between our movie and these happenings, nor could or would I point a finger of accusation at anyone. Suffice it to say, if someone had wanted to intimidate me via my family they had failed. But if their aim was to make me fed up with the whole stinking mess, enough to make me want to leave the film as quickly as I contractually could, they had succeeded. I wanted out so badly I could taste it.

16

Townshend
And Trouble

By late November, we had drawn up our plans for our next shooting sequence, which was to be a full concert somewhere in London. During this period, we had looked at a hall in Hemel Hempstead but the band decided not to have an advertised normal gig with a paying audience.

This was another of those periods when the band, the film crew and the management were all at odds with each other. Nothing was going right and everyone was pulling in different directions. There were three ways for things to go: the production company route, which was basically Sydney and me, with or without Bill, who made up his mind as he thought correct. Sometimes Roger would go with this track, and Keith would probably go along with it if he wasn't adversely affected. Then there was Jeff and his team, which included Eddie the editor and almost always had Pete as its mentor. By this stage, I had virtually nothing to do with Townshend. John didn't appear to want any part of these arguments and would go with the majority.

It was against this background that we were summoned to Ramport to talk about the concert. Also on the agenda were the sequence on John, to be shot at his country house in early January, and a studio segment in mid-December featuring the band's next album.

Who Are You? was the title of the next album and, as is usual with The Who, Townshend had made a demo of the entire thing, multi-tracking every instrument, the voices and harmonies. By this stage, I'd realised how little I'd ever known Townshend. Once rock's angry young man, he had seemingly become everything he'd once detested. He'd become a professional spokesman for the posers who, in becoming non-conformists in the late 1960s, had conformed to a new set of boring and ever more ridiculous codes of behaviour and dress rules, as strict as any army. Townshend wasn't such a young man any more.

I can't pretend we'd become close friends during the months we'd worked together on the film. In fact, I got the uncomfortable impression that he regarded my colleagues and me as paid help, kind of expensive roadies. Every once in a while he'd get curiously intense with me about something, but this usually followed a period of weeks when he wouldn't even say good morning.

We all knew the next album was past due, but the arguments and delays were crippling the band and tearing it apart. Basically, they've been arguing about the same thing for years, to tour or not to tour, Daltrey fighting like crazy to get back on the road, Townshend adamantly refusing. He wanted to be with his family in the privacy of his

Twickenham home, especially since the doctors had told him he'd need a course in lip-reading if he carried on performing at volume. One of the world's great rock performers going deaf, the ultimate irony. All those mums and dads who'd said rock music would do you harm would be delighted – vindication at last!

While we were in The Who's studio at the end of another long production meeting, Townshend looked at me pointedly and asked me to hang around as the rest of the film technicians and group personnel filed out. 'I want you to tell me what you think about this,' he said, then started the reel to reel and locked the door as the sound of 'Who Are You?' crashed into the room.

A good question, I thought, but said nothing. The music was good but not fantastic, pleasant but not shattering, adequate but not The Who… I kept quiet as Townshend sat and bopped to his own music, his eyes boring into mine, for some reason wanting my opinion at that moment. I was brought up not to say anything unless I had something good to say so I kept quiet as the last note died.

'Well then, Mr Producer, what do you think?' he asked aggressively.

'It's very good,' I responded after what seemed a decently lengthy pause for thought.

'*Very good?!!*' He exploded in rage. 'Very good! What does that mean? Tell me what you really think!' Now he was pacing the room.

'How old are you, Pete?'

'What's that got to do with anything?' he responded testily.

'Well, you're not a kid of 18 with nothing in his pockets – you can't have that despair in your heart, that hate or anger in your soul any more. I mean, you've got everything – a lovely family, houses, cars, businesses all over the place and you're still pretending to be this poor kid on the street, when you and him are two very different people –'

I hadn't finished when he started to scream obscenities at me, before ending with: 'What do you know about it, you stinking idiot?'

During the next nine months, Pete and I didn't speak. I can't say I missed a lot.

After Pete's outburst, I was never again sure how much of his anger was an affectation and how much was real. One very good pal told me how he was with Roger Daltrey after an American concert date, with the press in attendance. Into the dressing room came Pete, usually very reserved with my friend, but on this occasion he grabbed and hugged him, then engaged him in an animated conversation while the photographers happily snapped away. Two hours later, he was sitting at his hotel bar having a drink when Townshend entered. My friend said hello, but Pete totally ignored him and walked away.

Although we had arranged to film the group in their recording studio a day or two prior to the concert shoot, the band cancelled the filming at 6pm the night before. So we switched all our attention to the Kilburn State and it was in this grimy North London hall that the band were to perform before an audience for the first time in more than a year.

I was busy making last-minute arrangements when Sydney suggested we should wish them luck. We went up the dark concrete stairway and entered the dressing room. Some journalists were hovering around asking questions and it was obvious that everyone was nervous and edgy. Townshend sat alone, speaking to no one, brooding and withdrawn. John Entwistle was drinking brandy and seemed about ready to keel over. Keith Moon looked paunchy and ridiculous in an outsize Aladdin suit, while Daltrey talked to John Blake from the *Evening News*. I remember Roger's last statement before being called on stage: 'If any of us dropped out then we couldn't replace them. It just wouldn't be The Who any more.'

I sneaked another look at Pete and must admit to a feeling of guilt. He was heading towards being only a recording artist, happy with his family, looking after his health and here we were dragging the man back on stage. We calledout our best wishes and rushed down to our camera positions.

The hall was packed. Although the band, particularly Pete, didn't want an audience, I felt that for a Who performance to have real balls we had to have live bait, so I'd earlier called a radio station anonymously and told them there was to be a free Who concert that afternoon. Later, I discovered that one or two others on the production team had had the same idea. Minutes after the first DJ's broadcast, thousands of people were trying to break down the doors of the hall. I then had to phone the radio stations again to deny the rumour that I'd helped to create.

The band looked shocked as they dashed out on stage and

saw the big crowd but from the first chord of 'Can't Explain' it was as if they'd never been away. Townshend was leaping higher, looking meaner and leaner than ever. Daltrey was whirling his mike in enormously wide arcs. Moon was totally over the top, alternating between thumping his drums and his own head. Entwistle was very carefully not disturbing the brandy within.

After another five supercharged songs had been rattled off without pause, it became clear that Pete was becoming angry at a section of the audience – and at whoever had arranged for his band's exposure while still unrehearsed. He hurled an amplifier from the top of his stack and kicked a mike off the stage. 'I've got a guitar up here, unless any little big-mouthed fucking git wants to come up here and take it from me...' Suddenly the anger dissolved and he turned to Roger and grinned idiotically.

The band then roared into a powerhouse 'Summertime Blues' and the packed, sweaty hall shook with the audience's feet pounding in time to the music. Daltrey now stomped forward, his knees like pistons aimed at his chin. Head back, he poured out the lyrics. Entwistle's head turned like a slow hungry alligator, looking for meat. Moon, although flagging from fatigue, was still managing to thrash about in semi-madness, while Townshend's right hand swooped down, lacerating his fingers on sharp guitar strings, his running and jumping ever more frenetic. I watched and felt the power with an awe that has never left me since. It was a different side of the group I'd come to dislike through personal contact, but that night I realised that The Who's reality was out on stage, not in a recording studio. Their show was something more than a normal concert by any other artists I'd ever seen.

The chemistry between the band and their audience was a relationship of continual two-way feedback, ever increasing until you wanted to reach out and touch even if you'd get an electric shock. Other groups may start out close to their roots but the distance grows between them in direct ratio to the group's growing fame and success. Other groups become aloof and remote from their roots. But The Who, either by accident or design – and I think it's a mixture of both – have managed to keep themselves mentally at street level.

There was the usual row brewing between Daltrey and the rest, particularly Entwistle, because Roger couldn't hear himself sing above the bass. As always he was telling John to turn it down, but, unlike a famous night in Houston, John didn't throw his guitar on the floor and tell Roger to play the fucking thing. John always thought it was a much better idea for the band to smash up its equipment than each other.

As the concert came to its furious climax, Sydney shouted to me from a couple of feet away, 'This isn't a bad ten grand's worth, eh?'

I agreed: for under £10,000 we'd taken part in staging one of the best concerts of the entire year. The music finished to tumultuous applause and Jeff signalled us to go with him to catch the filming of the group backstage. We were just ahead of them as they pounded up the stairs. We were bubbling with excitement telling them how fantastic the show had been, but it was clear they didn't think that this was the case.

Moon half-tripped up the stairs, resulting in my being shoved to the wall. I pushed his bulky frame off me, but as we got into the dressing room John and Keith grabbed Sydney and lifted him off his feet and shoved him backwards into the wall, tapping his head quite hard. 'Hollow, I believe!' said Moon. It wasn't a vicious act, just over-exuberance, a release for the adrenaline still pumping in their veins.

There was an instant post-mortem of the concert, which the band thought had been at best OK, despite all our assurances that it had been much, much better than that. I've filmed quite a few groups in concert and I'd never seen a more exciting performance. It wasn't so much the quality as the sheer visceral power of the delivery.

The days after the Kilburn shoot were frustrating because, although the footage looked great to me, it didn't to Jeff, who was convinced we should reshoot most of, if not all, the material. Once again, he wasn't happy with the camera work, although this new team had followed his direction and were his handpicked men and had an outstanding reputation for technical and artistic excellence.

In particular, the lighting cameraman didn't seem able to believe the harsh criticism coming his way at the screening of the dailies. I felt a great deal of sympathy for the talented and engaging technician. He'd done his best, he had followed his instructions, he was very good at his job and he was being criticised. I made it my business to say thanks for a job well done, because sometimes the money just doesn't do it for you. Jeff didn't want this crew again. Eddie Rothkowitz, who was now in the cutting rooms, said, 'Maybe I'll be able to rescue some bits and pieces,' after he'd closely examined the rushes. Welcome to our Looking Glass world.

Eddie is a good editor I'm sure, because he continually told me so, but things that normally took me two or three days were taking our entire editorial staff as many weeks. The editing crew insisted that they needed additional custom-built cutting-room machines, which also meant an extra cutting room. This led to a couple of extra editorial assistants, which all together meant the editorial department had evolved into a burgeoning empire.

Our film schedule and cost also increased a lot because some of the production staff stood to receive an endless flow of salary and expenses if it continued at an ever-decreasing pace. I wanted the film in the cinemas quickly and offered to work for no extra fees if and when the film went over schedule, as long as all the rest of the film's executive staff would do the same! There were no other takers, which was surprising since it was supposedly me who was money mad. Bill was gratified by my offer, but I regretted it when he forgot the second part of it and felt that I alone should work for nothing while my playmates – the artists who cared only for the creation of excellence unsullied by that dirty green stuff – received their due extra payments.

On 20 December, we booked dates in mid-January for the start of our music mixes. In my ignorance I thought that meant the end might be nigh. We enjoyed a Christmas lunch in the Pinewood Studio restaurant with the entire production staff, who, despite growing divisions, managed to be friendly and convivial company. Jeff gave me a very smart grey cashmere scarf, which made me ashamed of the gaudy underpants I presented to him. Wine flowed and Jeff and I stopped the mutual point-scoring, which led to us both relaxing and having a good time, something that was never to be repeated.

17

The Ox And
The Skeletons

On 5 January, our growing circus checked into a sleepy hotel in Gloucestershire. The town was a quiet but lovely corner of England called Stow-on-the-Wold, as picturesque and quaint as its name implies. We were in this appealing backwater to film the John Entwistle sequence of our movie at his home near by.

The crew, with yet another new cameraman, arrived at John's house before noon. The term 'house' doesn't adequately describe the near-palatial dimensions of this mansion, set in its own huge green pastures and woods. I can't remember how many rooms there were but you could swing several large cats without hitting anything. John introduced us to his wife and delighted in showing us around while our technical staff set up the cameras and lights in the hallway and bar room.

Like Roger and Keith, John had created his own world of toys and pleasures. There was a state-of-the-art recording studio in one room and a seemingly endless supply of booze in the bar room, which was bigger than most London pubs despite having only one regular customer. The other abundance was John's giant collection of guitars – there must have been about a hundred of every type and description. Unlike Keith, who regarded his many gold discs as just a cheap form of wall covering, John stored most of his guitars out of sight. Jeff had them set up throughout the hallway and stairs so that he could film John walking past them in one shot.

Then it was out to the patio where John, now armed with a rifle, called, 'Pull!' and a gold disc was thrown up by one of the crew and then shot at by John, as if he was on a clay-pigeon shoot. Eventually out of feigned frustration John used a machine gun to shatter the golden airborne records. John seemed to have fun playing at the manic country squire – you could tell by a slight twitch of a smile on his taciturn face. I don't know who had given him the nickname of The Ox but perhaps The Statue would have been more appropriate. He was so stiff and uptight with everything around him. Jeff and I tried without much success to loosen him up, because otherwise this section of the film would reflect this uncomfortable attitude, made worse when compared to the loose and ready spontaneity of the rest of the group.

Jeff had one of his more inspired ideas when, after he'd started a boozy, late-night interview with John, the camera pulled back to reveal that the people he was talking to were in fact skeletons. John was so enamoured by his new friends that he bought them for a couple of hundred pounds after the filming. John undoubtedly has a dark sense of humour, which was more easily identifiable after several drinks at about 2am. However, try as I might, I can't remember anything of note that he said, humorous or otherwise. Extracting conversation from him was like drawing teeth.

When John was away from his home environment, he could party with the best. He could out-drink, out-romance and out-loon almost anyone. But at home he became very much the lord of the manor, talking about the most mundane things at great length in boring detail.

John had worked for the Inland Revenue and his attitudes towards money seemed to reflect that institution's desire to collect as much as possible. His reply to a question about the group's success was illuminating. 'We became rich and famous a bit later than I expected – now I'm too old to enjoy my money,' he said, smiling wistfully. John's one consuming passion in relation to the film was his demand that he should have as much time, effort and money expended on his section as that lavished on the other members of the group. This was to my mind a reasonable demand; less so was the looming possibility that he'd also demand equal screen time in the final film, although this could well screw the balance of the movie. He just wasn't as exciting, interesting or entertaining on screen as his colleagues.

John was determined to tell us about his composing contribution to the group and he also spoke with pride about his own group, aptly named Mortis. More interesting to me was the fact that it was John and Keith who'd first dreamed up the idea of a group called Led Zeppelin, which they were going to form with a couple of the guys who did eventually participate in that band. That occurred, according to John, during one of the legendary bust-ups within The Who. 'I sometimes wish we'd have done it,' he said, 'things would have been a bit different if we had.'

Although the band were always at each other's throats in public and sniping at one another in private, if an outsider ever tried to have a go they would become a tightly knit unit against the world. John was as much a part of the whole as any of the other three, the binding glue and the necessary solid counterweight to the lunatic antics of his cohorts.

Daltrey described the unusual nature of the band when he said, 'We're not a four-piece band, we're a four-million-piece band.' This kind of statement is a more pleasant, self-effacing side of the band's attitude to rock than Pete's, who was liable at any time to say some unbelievably pompous nonsense about rock's part in the world. Of course, it's everyone's right to voice an opinion but Pete's ideas had so overwhelmed those of the other three that each of them compensated for this imbalance in their own way.

John talked into the night about some of his ideas for a more ornate, sophisticated sound for The Who. 'It would be nice to be able to hear the bass properly for a change,' he added. 'I'll have to get involved with the music mixes for the film, otherwise old cloth-ears Pete will screw it up. We'll make sure we can hear that bass nice and clear.' He took another sip from his glass and toasted the skeleton while the cameras resumed filming.

The next day's work was much the same. John was now more comfortable in our company and unwound to the extent that he was able to let the cameras see a bit more behind his carefully constructed defensive shell. His brain was obviously good when he allowed it to surface.

However, he was a difficult character to know or to film, which led us to create one of the less satisfactory portions of our movie. I don't believe we ever overcame his basic reticence to discover what his innermost thoughts were, so we had placed him in fun situations that didn't really suit his personality. These ill-fitting scenes did nothing to enhance the film or to do justice to John. I believe he felt much the same way, although I can't claim to hear him saying so directly. We can't blame John for our failings; as the film's makers we should have been able to construct a better platform for him.

8 JANUARY 1978, NEW YORK

After filming the Entwistle sequence, I left for America and another hunt for library material. Sydney had gone a day earlier and we left the preliminary music mix-downs in the hands of Jeff and the editing staff. While we were out of the country, we found out that the cutting rooms had been entirely moved to the West End of London. Once again, while the cat was away the mice were playing. When we got back from the US, there was a letter from the film's accountants, attacking us with the fact that the move had taken place without their knowledge and would obviously cost money that hadn't been allowed for in the budget — exactly the sort of thing I'd been saying before we left, and had been agreed with, on the surface at least, by Bill.

Five days before we left, Jeff had made the point that the film couldn't be assembled until we'd delivered all the outstanding library material, which was still under negotiation in America — hence our trip. This was Jeff's first formal indication that the blame for lack of progress with the film lay with us.

Here is an extract from my memo to the office from that trip. These normally confidential papers cover a small part of what happens when someone in the film business goes on one of these trips. They're actually working very hard.

7–27 JANUARY, USA TRIP

In reference to the following report, two fundamental points are raised:

1. All material required by everyone on the production is now either in England or en route to England.
2. In relation to possible film sales deals on our movie, it is apparent that there is a great and growing interest from the major corporations for both North America and the rest of the world. However, it must be borne in mind by us all that all the parties to these conversations made the point that the sale would be contingent upon their liking what they see and hear once we have something to show them. Stating the obvious, if they do not like it they won't buy it.

We still feel confident that, if the show reel does measure up to our expectations, these major corporations will bid for the film in competition with each other and our trip in early March to sell the film will be successful.

One of the most important facets of the trip for both Sydney Rose and Tony Klinger was the meetings with four major studios in respect of distribution in US/Canada (and possibly the world). The studios and parties involved were as follows:

1. G. Wigan — 20th Century Fox
2. Jeff Katzenberg — Paramount Picture Corporation
3. Ned Tanen — Universal
4. Larry Marks — Warner Brothers

20TH CENTURY FOX

Basically their attitude was that they would like to see a rough assembly and would consider distribution for the US and Canada, although they questioned the possibility of worldwide distribution. They would be prepared to work out a deal with or without a soundtrack album, but obviously they would like us to consider their record company, 20th Century Records, which they even admitted themselves was not the best record company in the world, but, due to its recent success with the *Star Wars* album, they felt they could be of some use in this field. It was also stated by Tony Klinger that we would not want to have a cross-collateralisation situation with various territories, etc. and, should we discuss a worldwide distribution with them, we would have to agree on fixed guarantees for the various territories in question.

As we all know, 20th Century Fox have a tremendous amount of cash, mainly due to *Star Wars*, and are very anxious to have a screening of our assembly as soon as possible. It was noted from our investigations that 20th Century have one of the best press and publicity departments in Hollywood. It was left for Sydney Rose and Tony Klinger to get back to Fox in order to set up a screening date in LA as we were not prepared to screen anything here in London for Sandy Lieberson, who could only say 'no' or refer it back to the West Coast, and for this reason alone it is essential that the screening should be at Fox as soon as our rough assembly in 35mm and a portfolio on the film is ready.

PARAMOUNT

Basically the meeting with Jeff Katzenberg was the same as for Fox, except they informed me prior to my [SR] leaving for London that they would want to see something longer than a rough assembly of say 30 minutes. However, it is the general feeling that, if their competitors are going to make a bid on a 20–25mm rough assembly, then Paramount would want to be included in the ball game.

In view of Paramount's fantastic success with *Saturday Night Fever* which has grossed $41m in 41 days and with their forthcoming product which includes further music/rock orientated films, i.e. *Grease*, *American Hot Wax*, etc. they feel they are the 'right' company for *The Kids Are Alright*. The soundtrack situation with Paramount could be either CBS, RSO or A&M: three companies which they work very closely with and have had enormous success of late.

UNIVERSAL

Ned Tanen wanted to see the film and was very interested. However, it was the opinion of both Sydney Rose and Tony Klinger that, as Ned Tanen would be the main point of contact for *The Kids Are Alright* and as he was supervising at least 10–12 other films, we felt that, although Universal must not be discounted, they go right to the bottom of the list. Naturally, should the deal go with Universal, the soundtrack would be on MCA Records, which obviously The Who are under contract to. After leaving Ned Tanen's office we reported our meeting to Lou Cook of MCA Records and the sum total of his attitude was with special reference to the soundtrack album that MCA Records would 'fight' for the soundtrack album of *The Kids Are Alright*. Lou Cook also made the comment that Pete Townshend may or may not feel that we have a soundtrack album for the film.

WARNER BROTHERS

Sydney Rose had a meeting with Larry Marks of some one and a half hours' duration whereupon the concept, distribution and overall promotion ideas were discussed at great length. Larry Marks on behalf of Warner Bros is extremely interested in the distribution of *The Kids Are Alright*, in view of their previous experience with Led Zeppelin's *The Song Remains the Same* and, of course, *Woodstock*. Larry Marks confirmed to Sydney Rose that he would like to see a rough assembly of some 25–30 mins as soon as possible, together with a written concept plus a portfolio of information on the film. At such a screening, he would have with him his other associates at Warner Bros who could make a decision about a deal on the spot. Sydney Rose mentioned to Larry Marks the minimum figure one would be talking about, i.e. the negative cost of $4m, and the fact that there was to be a soundtrack album which Warner Brothers Records would be extremely interested in. Larry Marks would contact Mo Austin, the head of Warner Bros Records to get his feelings.

COLUMBIA

Sal Iannucci had suggested to Sydney Rose and Tony Klinger that as Columbia Pictures had already distributed *Tommy* he felt they should not be discounted and, in fact, he made overtures on our behalf to Norman Levy, who had a considerable budget for the purpose of buying completed films for Columbia.

On the day of my departure for London, Sal Iannucci telephoned me at the hotel with the news that he had had a long conversation with Norman Levy and that Levy would like to see our rough assembly and portfolio, etc. on our next trip to LA in addition to meeting the aforementioned majors, i.e. Fox, Paramount, Universal and Warner Brothers.

During a discussion with Jeff Stein and Ed Rothkowitz of 7 February, Sydney Rose enquired as to the exact date or thereabouts of the next trip to LA, as Sydney had promised the major distributors a minimum of 14 days' notice prior to the trip. The date in question, given by Ed Rothkowitz, after Jeff Stein had to leave the meeting, was around 15/16 March, subject to major hold-ups.

Bill Curbishley and Sydney Rose will be lunching on Thursday, 9 February to discuss the latest position on *The Kids Are Alright* with special reference to this progress report, the forthcoming trip to LA for screenings with the majors, and discussions on our possible participation at the Cannes Film Festival in May, which both Sydney Rose and Tony Klinger feel would be an essential 'plus' to our overall plans.

The only thing out of all this that worked out in the end was that MCA did end up with the soundtrack album of the movie.

18

Onwards To
The Wilderness

As my period of first-call duty on the film drew towards its conclusion, I felt progressively more like what the Soviets called a 'non-person'. I could see that everyone, not least Jeff and Eddie, were relieved about my imminent departure. The atmosphere at the new cutting rooms in Dean Street was hostile and electric when Sydney and I went to meetings there or to view cuts. It became so tense one day that a can of film was flung at Sydney for no apparent reason.

The cutting-room staff were in a state of constant anxiety and the progress of the cutting itself was slow. The pace, which had never been speedy, had become glacial. Jeff once said to Sydney in jest, 'Come up and we'll let you see the frame we've got for you. It's a very good frame.'

It had become usual on our production for no one to be very enthusiastic about the results of our latest shoot, and Jeff immediately talked about wanting to do a reshoot with

John Entwistle. But, as I was taking a step back from running the show, the knives were now being sharpened for Sydney, who was about to suffer like no one should.

By late January, the famous French TV clips, which we had been told didn't exist, had finally arrived, but the budget for all the extra shooting Jeff wanted to undertake – in 35mm instead of the 16mm we'd been using – had not. We had agreed it in theory but in practice we didn't have the extra money from an already unhappy band.

As a result, about £90,000 of these extra shoots were dropped by early February. This meant there weren't going to be any special interviews with either Daltrey or Townshend, nor such gems as a Who devastation spectacular, in which an ornate columned set was to collapse by the end of their finale. It's symbolic of the film that some of the items that could have made it a bigger commercial success weren't produced because of lack of funding, while hundreds of thousands were in my view wasted on rubbish.

A prime example of this extravagance was the way our music mixes began to take shape. The studios we were using for this work were in Wembley, North London. Present were Jeff, Eddie and a few of his crew, sometimes Sydney, me, Cy Langston from the Who's inner circle and John Entwistle.

The problems flowed from the fact that Eddie correctly wanted these new mixes to be run in a fairly organised, film-making manner, whereas our music director – John – felt more comfortable working in the relaxed style of a

Who recording session. The way this worked in practice was that the film people would arrive at noon, spend a few hours in general preparation, have a bite to eat, then await the music guys who'd show up later in the afternoon or early evening. We'd then work to one or two o'clock the next morning.

Although the studio was a handsome modern structure, it soon began to feel more like a prison than a place of work. It was obvious that John and Cy looked at the film only in a musical context and never fully understood the filmic requirements. For this reason, yet another split evolved, this time between the film technicians and the music experts, who each thought the others complete idiots. Feelings and tempers grew steadily worse with each session, although most of the time we managed to retain a veneer of cool politeness to one another.

Making matters worse was the claustrophobic nature of Studio Four, where this work was undertaken. The mixing room itself wasn't a bad size but three-quarters of its space was taken up by the huge mixing console and its back-up equipment. Added to this clutter were our TV monitors for visual playback and about ten staff, all tripping over each other in the narrow, dimly lit spaces between the low Scandinavian leather armchairs and everything else. On top of all that there would be extremely loud rock music played over and over again in the middle of the night, a lot of stale cigarette smoke hanging in the air, and too much wine and beer being drunk. Half the crew were speedy on cocaine, while others were mellowed out on grass. None of this would totally destroy a music session but it was a recipe for problems.

Further, on day one the studio sound system went down, leaving us to watch the studio's head technician sort out the gremlins for a couple of hours before we could even start. It was an inauspicious start for what would become one of the film's major hang-ups, the sound mixes.

Sounds on a film like this one are an extremely important but complex ingredient of the finished product. When filming, you also record the sound from the location or studio. This gives you the actors speaking; everything else – wind rustling the trees, the leaves cracking, footsteps walking, clothing rustling, some bells in the distance, a dog barks near by, a stair creaks, a door opens – is usually added on later. You then mix all these and other created sounds with the original track of the actors' voices and add music – all of which must be balanced so that you, the audience, hear the whole sound as you imagine it would be in everyday circumstances. As our movie was primarily a musical extravaganza, our rock music had to sound right to the sophisticated modern ear. What was acceptable 15 years ago on a hand-held transistor radio would now sound awful over powerful modern speakers.

Therefore, it was essential to make our older music sound good, but equally we needed to keep the flavour of its original format, ready for an eventual Dolby stereo dub. Finding an acceptable balance between the original rawness on some of those raunchy, sometimes tinny early tracks and the later, almost over-produced sounds of the band proved quite a task. John eventually accomplished it brilliantly; so well, in fact, that most people who saw the film or heard the album never realised what a major job John had done.

If true art can be defined as being that which looks effortless, John managed some art in that studio. He managed to retain the original flavour while making the sound quality acceptable to the first-time listener. It just took a long time to achieve. Our first mix-downs took 112 hours and 45 minutes, spread over ten days.

Halfway through the first night as we sat listening to a nearly complete track pounding out of the massive speakers, I knew for certain that in reality we were preparing a record first and a film music track second. 'It's a shame,' I said to John, 'that this isn't going to be an album. A lot of kids are going to want to hear this stuff who don't have the early albums.'

John looked at me as if I were insane. 'Of course there's gonna be an album. What do you think I'm playing at here?'

'I thought Pete didn't want an album of the film,' I replied.

'Well, he doesn't lay down the rules, does he? He's only one out of four of us. Of course there'll be an album.'

I didn't bother going into the details of why I'd made my statement but I noticed Sydney and Jeff making mute gestures indicating we should talk, so we went outside to the cold damp winter air of the car park. As we leaned on its iron railings, Sydney spoke first, the air from his mouth forming small puffs of warm whiteness. 'So now we know for certain, there is going to be an album.'

'You didn't ever believe there wasn't going to be an album, did you?' asked Jeff.

'Just so long as we all get something for ourselves, it's fine,' I said. 'Otherwise, the film which we do have a piece of is costing more than it should, because we must be spending twice as much on this mix as we would just for a film. The band can't have it both ways.'

There was general accord on this but none of us had much idea how we were going to do anything about it. After another ten minutes or so of aimless chat, we went back into the studio.

I had just gone to the corner to fetch some coffee when Jeff, who was standing behind John at the mixing console, beckoned me over. 'Tony, I think you'd like to see this.'

I started in their direction and saw Eddie, who was sitting next to John, lean in closer to look at something John was doodling. Both Eddie and Jeff were ashen-faced. The whole studio went quiet in one moment – so much so that Sydney, who'd been leafing through some papers from his briefcase, looked up to find out why. We both came up behind John at the same moment and saw the drawing he'd just finished.

It was a cartoon of a cinema entrance made to look like the archway of a concentration camp. On the arch, instead of the Nazi legend *Arbeit Macht Frei* [Work sets you free] were the words 'Are the Yids all right?' Walking under this arch were four figures, which clearly were Stein, Rothkowitz, Rose and me. In the background of the drawing was a building from which a long chimney was billowing smoke. We were all silent, struck dumb by the crude anti-Semitic nature of the cartoon. John was obviously unaware of this because his next words were, 'The only trouble with cinemas these days is that they don't have enough gas ovens for all the Jews.'

'That's not very funny, John,' Jeff said.

Entwistle looked up and immediately realised the extent to which he'd upset us. I can't speak for the others but personally I'm not religious. I'm Jewish by race and proud of it. I'd belonged to an anti-Nazi group whose aim it was to fight neo-Nazis wherever we could find them. From those insane thugs and butchers I could understand and expect such an appalling insult, such depth of venom, such unreasoning insensibility, but from a supposedly enlightened and sophisticated world traveller as John Entwistle it was hard to fathom, and very hurtful.

'You know we're Jewish, John. Do you think we'd find that funny?'

John picked up the drawing, crumpled it up into a tight little ball and threw it into the wastepaper basket. 'C'mon, I didn't mean anything by it, you berks. It was just a joke,' he said.

'It was a pretty lousy joke,' said Eddie.

'I'm going for a drink. Anybody want to come?' John asked.

None of us went with him.

'Another bloody anti-Semite,' said Sydney when John had left the room.

'I think it was just a bad joke, fellas,' said Jeff. 'Sometimes he's a bit dumb.'

'Really,' I said. 'If he doesn't like Jews he's not in the right business. Films and music are full of them, and if he ever pulled a stunt like that with them he could wave his career goodbye.'

'It's not worth talking about,' Eddie said. 'He's just a dumb ox; otherwise, he wouldn't have said it.'

We all went to grab something to eat from the sandwich tray but, apart from some banter to try to lighten the atmosphere, we kept our own counsel on our innermost reactions.

A little later, I said to Sydney, 'I can't work with the prick any more tonight. I'm going home. I don't think I'll come back to work with him again either. What about you, Sydney?'

Sydney also got up. 'Yeah, I think I'll go home too. They can get by without us. Goodnight, Jeff, goodnight, Eddie.'

'Someone's got to stay,' Jeff said as we began to leave. 'Goodnight, guys.'

'Yeah, goodnight,' I replied. 'Let's get some T-shirts printed that say, "The Yids Are Alright" and we'll make sure we've got one that fits John.'

'Yeah,' said Eddie, 'we'll get John's made out of black leather — he'd like that!'

At least we all had a wry smile on our faces as we split.

We did spend another couple of nights in the studio but I kept my distance from John and took no part in anything other than film-business talk with him. He seemed oblivious to this and I feel he genuinely didn't know how deeply his actions had cut. If you wanted to design a schedule of actions to screw up hearts and minds and deter any empathy, you'd have to acknowledge the band and their merry men as masters of the art.

On these unannounced visits of mine to the studio, it was quite obvious that several of our crew were high on cocaine – not John, but some of the technical staff were cutting lines in the toilet every half-hour or so. I couldn't do anything unless it visibly affected that person's performance, but one day I was called aside by the studio manager, who I knew well from previous film music sessions. 'Tony, you've got to do something quickly about these drugs. The police have been called by someone. I just found out, and we don't want an arrest here, do we? Especially with John around.'

Just as he finished speaking, Townshend came down the corridor and barely mumbled hello in our direction. I rushed into the studio and whispered the news I'd just heard in a few ears; there was much toilet flushing as several packets of incriminating substances were disposed of.

'Here he is, the harbinger of doom,' said Townshend, slumped moodily in his seat looking at me through hooded slit eyes.

I looked around at the group of people I'd been spending all of the year with and I realised I had to be either mad or a masochist. I observed Townshend listening to Entwistle's sound mixes and watched my colleagues knocking each other over to brown-nose both of them. It wasn't an appealing sight. I became determined to use this experience as a guide for my future. I'd never be so weak or soft in business again. I'd learn my lessons well from these masters.

As we tried to ready the showreel for the American major

distributors, it became ever more apparent we weren't going to meet our deadlines. I decided that my priorities were two-fold. First, I had to make one last attempt to ensure the film was a success. Second, I prepared what I believed was a fair budget that would accurately reflect the costs of the film, both past and future. All the other costs had simply been lumped on to the original budget I'd prepared, which in reality was for a very different film to the new version we were making. When this comprehensive costing was unveiled at just under three-quarters of a million pounds, I pointed out that this figure didn't include any money for library footage, The Who's in-house costs or, more importantly, any major advertising and distribution costs.

Jeff was incredulous at the size of my budget, although I had prepared it based on comprehensive discussions I'd had with him on his future plans. Jeff told me that he and Eddie were sure that I'd needlessly inflated these figures to attack them by implication, and they couldn't foresee the picture costing more than about £625,000. I was desperately anxious to make it plain to everyone that these costs were not what I'd like to see happen, but the reality of what was going to happen, at best.

At worst, I could easily imagine a doom-laden scenario taking longer and costing far more. I appealed to Bill for a mass meeting with the whole band and all the film's senior staff, but he also said my figures didn't make any sense because they were too high. The band simply wouldn't come up with all the extra funding required, so to speak with them about it would be a waste of their time.

I'd become so distanced from the band by this time that I didn't even pick up the telephone to any of them to voice my fear for our film and their money. I should have but I was so screwed up and confused by some of their previous unfavourable reactions to my actions that I no longer had any faith in their ability to act objectively with regards to our film or myself. We needed one hundred per cent of The Who's artistic involvement and moral commitment, not purely monetary support; I never felt we had it, any of it, even when they were together in front of the cameras. If Pete wanted to go for something, Roger would be pulling in the other direction and the opposite also held true.

During our production, the band's commitment to each other, let alone the film, was stretched paper-thin, and the tensions of not knowing what they were going to do next were just too much to deal with. It didn't make it easier for me to realise that the band didn't know what came next either, nor did their management, lawyers or record companies. Instead of the film being a vehicle for the enjoyment of us all, particularly the band, it had evolved in a way none of us could have desired or foreseen except in our darkest nightmares. The band should have been in a position to bathe in the glow of their achievement during a film celebrating their past, which in turn could have been a launching pad to an exhilarating future full of new challenges. Instead, I could see we might be acting as gravediggers at a macabre artistic and financial burial of The Who.

I did send Roger a handwritten letter trying to set the record straight but I never received any response, so I don't know if he got it or if he just didn't think it worthy of reply. Of course, the film was now desperately short of funds, which meant Sydney's company was under increasing pressure from the film's creditors, who didn't want to know about reasons but simply wanted their money. This was the squeeze situation I had warned Sydney about when I'd turned down the option of allowing my company to be used as the vehicle for the production.

Now we were faced with a major set of problems, and whenever Sydney had decisions to make he was forced to sit on the fence by money worries. He was terrified that any action he took might offend The Who or their management and that they would cut off the already insufficient money coming to him, without which his company would go into immediate bankruptcy.

Our most heated meeting yet took place on 28 February in Bill's offices. In theory, we had come in to discuss the new budget, which Bill wanted reduced. You can probably visualise my jaw dropping open at Bill's opening statement. 'We're putting ourselves – that's the boys and me – down for £300,000 in deferred fees. Plus we'll have to put something down for John and our other technical guys, like Cy Langston, for their work on the music mixes – say another £30,000 to £40,000. So you can put that lot in your budget, Klinger.'

Sydney went white and I imagine I did too. Not even Bill could think we'd just mutely accept this unwarranted, illegitimate and unilateral breach of our contracts. This series of payments and deferments would dilute my piece of the action and Sydney's, making them valueless unless the film grossed a fortune.

Our percentages had been calculated and agreed in contracts, against a set production cost. For example, if the film's cost was £500,000 and it grossed £5,000,000 at the cinemas, we would get our money from the last figure minus the first figure, minus the cinemas' share, distributors' percentage, advertising costs, prints of the film, publicity, shipping charges, customs clearances, sales commissions, etc. These items could amount to a total on this film of about £4,250,000. Now add in the original cost of production – £500,000 – and our total outgoings would be £4,750,000 against total revenues of £5,000,000, which would leave only £250,000 to be divided between The Who, Jeff, Sydney and myself.

If, on top of all those deductions, The Who managed to skim off another £330,000 by adding their fees to our budget, it would mean no one else's agreed percentages had any real chance of being worthwhile. We were being carved up in the worst way.

'You can't do that, Bill,' I replied quietly and carefully. 'That's not fair and it's not right.'

'I don't give a toss what you think about it, Klinger. I'm not asking you, I'm telling you that's what the boys are gonna get for their work on the film.'

'Bill,' Sydney interjected, 'you know nothing was in the budget for the boys because they got an extra large share of the profits instead.'

Bill grew angrier. 'Well, now they'll have both, won't

they, Sydney? Why should they be the only people working for nothing on this picture?'

'Bill,' I said, 'number one, we've got a contract that stipulated who gets what, which everyone has signed. Second, the band aren't getting nothing – they own about 75 per cent of this bloody picture. If you get away with putting down an extra £300,000 or £400,000 in fees, even if most of them are deferred, it's just a device to make sure none of us with a percentage of profits ever gets anything. I'm not going to accept it.'

'What can you do about it?' Bill asked. 'You're off first call next week 'cos you're such a busy boy on your other picture. Anyway, your contract's with Sydney's company, and I don't think he's going to go along with you because I'm going to look after Sydney because he's loyal to this film. I'm gonna pay him a good bonus for staying on, so the only way you could do anything is to sue Sydney's company. So you have a good time, because I'm telling you what's going to happen whether you like it or not.'

I got up from my chair and addressed Sydney. 'I'm going because there's no point in talking about this any more, and I can see Bill's not in a mood to listen.'

'Don't be silly, Tony,' Sydney replied. 'I'm sure we can sort this out.'

'How?' I asked. 'You're just being told that we can stick our contracts up our arse.'

Bill, now seemingly calmer, spoke again. 'I never said anything like that. I'm just saying the boys have to get their fair whack.'

I sat down again and leaned forward in my seat. 'Bill, I don't accept any of these new additions to the budget you've just made, but as I'm off the picture on first call next week I think I should stay to straighten the rest of this budget out.'

Once again, Bill reacted volcanically. 'Well, I don't think I want to discuss it with you if you're walking away from the film.'

'Bill, you've known about me having another film to go to for nearly six months,' I retorted. 'I've already stayed on this picture two or three months longer than we originally anticipated it would take to make the whole bloody thing. So how you can imply I'm walking as if it were a surprise staggers me.'

Bill said very quietly, 'If I see you in court, Klinger, you'll be torn apart.'

'Bill, if I have to, I'll take every penny you've paid me to sue you with if you go through with this nonsense.'

I got up and walked from the room, leaving Sydney with Bill to discuss the budget I'd prepared.

I was plainly out in the wilderness and alone. I felt I was being made the whipping boy for all the film's problems and, as I wouldn't be around to protect my back much longer, I knew with absolute certainty that until the underlying truth of my statements were vindicated in the fullness of time I would be everyone's villain. By that time, of course, it would be too late to do anything to rectify the situation.

3 MARCH 1978

On my last day of first-call duty on the production, I wrote two lengthy letters to Sydney, laying down all the facts and opinions I've referred to. Also, it had come to my attention that there had just been a screening of the showreel for Bill, which Sydney and I weren't even told about. Apart from being bloody rude on Bill and Jeff's part, this was an absolutely nutty way to behave, since it was Sydney and I who had been rowing the sales boat and were the people who were readying the American majors to see this showreel. How could we be expected to contribute in any other meaningful way if we weren't allowed to see anything?

There was now no one on the production side of the picture in any position to plan or budget for the future. How could we, when we didn't know what was happening in the present? As I wrote in my letter to Sydney, 'I still do not understand how one is supposed to budget correctly or schedule anything on this film when the group is only prepared to be filmed when it suits them, although this contradicts your contract with them and the director tells us on a "need to know" basis only the information for action he thinks we require. In other words, we don't even know what he wants to shoot and when, for how long or with whom, or whether it's in 35mm or 16mm, whether he has spoken with the group without us or whether having agreed all these things, which has never been the case, Bill Curbishley might not override us for reasons of his own, which we are not privy to...'

They had bought a dog to bark but now Bill and Jeff wanted to make the barking noises themselves. As I'd begun to leave Bill's office on the 28th, he'd asked me who I thought was responsible for the problems of our film. 'First, Stein,' I'd said, 'then The Who, then you, Rock Films and last Sydney and me, in that order.'

He didn't reply immediately but after a moment he said, 'It's always someone else's fault, isn't it, Klinger? Never your own.'

'Bill,' I said, 'there will come a time sooner or later when you'll realise that Sydney and I have been telling you the truth and the right way to go all along. There's nothing we can do if you won't listen. I've told you a million times you can't give someone responsibility without authority.'

We were on two different roads and neither of us had the same map. We had got to a stage on the film when there was virtually no sensible communication between me and anyone else on it. Could everyone be wrong except myself? I thought so then and still do.

My first-call period ended without further drama and foolishly I presumed my hurly-burly days were over. Hard-edged views immediately became slightly blurred by a tinge of nostalgia as I left the office I'd been working in for so long to take up my new quarters at the other end of Pinewood Studios in the *Rock On* production suite.

My new seat wasn't yet warm when Sydney telephoned me to say that almost the entire film was being shipped at once to Los Angeles. We'd talked of sending a showreel but now it appeared we were sending everything we had, some

43,743 feet of film and sound still in its fairly raw state. This meant Sydney would be left with yet more egg on his face with the majors; no one knew when our travelling circus would have its act together. Not only was the showreel taking longer than scheduled, but it was also costing more than any of us could believe. Diverting all of this energy, time and money to it meant that no one had their eye on the ball, which still had to be getting the film itself finished.

Now our cutting rooms in London were in limbo because the senior staff and a great chunk of the film were in America. Neither entity could work without the other. The American companies were becoming nervous at the delays in seeing anything from us and increasingly wanted to see and hear more. They were all still eager to see something but it was becoming apparent that something was amiss on our picture, and nobody wants to buy expensive problems.

11 April 1978

Over lunch, Jeff questioned Sydney on the budget I'd prepared in February. Sydney told me that Jeff openly attacked this document and myself, demanding to know how these dramatic increases in costs were arrived at. Sydney said that he'd told Jeff the truth. 'You were involved in compiling material for that budget, Jeff. It takes account of everything we've already spent, plus all the things everybody still wants to do. If you speed up the finishing work, we could save some money, but otherwise the budget makes sense to me.'

This reply didn't seem to placate Jeff, who still thought the budget 'sucked', according to the notes I kept of Sydney's calls to me.

A few days later, Eddie Rothkowitz added to the derision of anything I did. Apparently, he said to one of the film's accountants, Sandy Singh, 'What kind of production is this, when the editor's got to work out the budgets and the producers should be back at school learning basic math?' Eddie had worked out a revised budget at Jeff's request.

It now became crystal clear that any edifice I'd had a part in building was being dismantled. The production personnel I hired were being dismissed or had resigned. The hostility from Jeff, Eddie and Bill was so sharply directed in my direction you could almost touch it. Not one day passed by without my receiving calls and memos from someone on *The Kids* warning me that I was under attack for something or other. Sydney told me it was his opinion that Bill really aimed to get the producer's credit on the film.

Sydney's company was now at a zero balance in the bank with huge debts mounting up. The pressures on him were immense from several directions. He had energetically and efficiently undertaken the mountainous task of locating and obtaining library material. Almost no one I knew, including myself, would have shown the patience and the sheer methodical persistence that Sydney had shown in obtaining so much library footage.

Sydney told me that he had been invited to join a meeting with Bill, Jeff and the group the next day but at the last minute he was told by Bill not to appear, since this might cause friction. I met with Sydney and told him I was sure he'd been targeted for dismissal and it was only a matter of time till he found life so intolerable that he'd quit. If not, sooner or later he'd be sacked.

Now schedules were emanating from Bill's office, which was taking over many of Sydney's duties and responsibilities. The first call sheet prepared since I had gone on to second call was prepared for a couple of days' filming at Shepperton. This was going to be a partial reshoot of the Kilburn gig, which Jeff didn't seem to like, even though the performance had had the music critics reinstating The Who as the live rock act of the year. The call sheet had one interesting omission – my name. It had been deleted, but before I could do anything about it Sydney had the error corrected and a new version was issued.

I'd have given almost anything to confront the band behind closed doors at this stage of the game. Even if they didn't deserve the truth, they would have got it from me. Now I knew the paramount reason for Jeff's private meetings with them was to continue pouring money into the production.

Shortly prior to the Shepperton filming date, Bill asked me to his office for a meeting. As I walked in, Bill said, 'I wasn't sure you'd come now that you're not on the film any more.'

'Bill, second call doesn't mean I'm not on the film,' I replied, 'just that my first obligation is elsewhere. If I'm needed here I'll come. I'm not finished here yet, you know that.'

'Well, if you're on this production, why don't you ever pick up the fucking phone and call me?' Bill asked.

'I could say the same thing, Bill. When I was on first call I tried calling you a million fucking times and it always took forever to get a call returned. You bloody well know I've offered my help time after time in any way it was needed.'

Bill looked towards Jeff who was sitting to his right, directly in front of me. 'You know, Jeff's like me in one way – he feels this film from the gut, but you and Sydney only see this thing from your brains. You're both like mobile adding machines.'

I couldn't believe the crap I was hearing. 'That's bullshit, Bill,' I said, 'but, if it weren't, I would say that from brains comes thought and the only thing that comes from your gut is shit. Perhaps that's why we've got so many problems on this film.'

Bill smiled at this reply, but Jeff looked even more sulky. What Bill said next took me totally by surprise. 'I'd like you to come back on the film, Tony, and do another comprehensive new budget. I'm going to California over the weekend but you ring me there Monday or Tuesday so that I can get together the necessary funding.' Then he paused and stood up. 'Why don't you come into my office for a while?' He started to leave the room, followed by Sydney. 'Just Tony, thank you, Sydney.'

We went alone into his room and sat down. 'Look, you know things are in a bit of a mess,' he began. 'We're gonna need you for the preparation and shoots coming up or we're gonna be totally in the shit. You'll get your pay for it or I'll have to hire someone else to fill in.'

I didn't gloat or say I told you so, however tempting it was. Instead, I said, 'Bill, I've told you I'm available to you for important stuff when I'm not shooting elsewhere, so of course I'll do it. I'll ring you in California as soon as I've got the figures done.'

We left it at that, and having re-established a friendlier rapport I wished him bon voyage and left.

I spent some considerable time working alone at home on the figures for the supposedly definitive budget. Having started again from scratch, I still came out at approximately the same place: about three-quarters of a million pounds or more.

During that time, I received a phone call from a guy I knew vaguely through my dad. His name was Jeremy Thomas, then a respected young film producer. He told me that Bill had appointed him 'creative consultant' on the film as of that day and he thought we should get together to discuss the film's past. So did I, as I had no idea of his status and how it affected me, Sydney or our film.

Jeremy was just a touch older than me, and he was to become a leading British film producer, founding the Recorded Picture Company and producing some terrific films, including Bernardo Bertolucci's *The Last Emperor*, which won the 1988 Academy Award for Best Picture. His father was the film director Ralph Thomas, who had directed many of the *Doctor* series of comedy films, while his uncle Gerald Thomas directed many of the *Carry On* films.

Jeremy, a cherubic-looking guy with curly hair and a

ready smile, came to my house and we spent a few hours discussing everything. I voiced my misgivings regarding the way he'd been appointed without my being informed, let alone asked, at the same time as I had been re-enlisted on the active duty by Bill. Nevertheless, it was obviously better to have a professional on the picture who I could get along with.

Jeremy had already been in consultation with Jeff and felt he could work well with him and couldn't understand my reservations in that regard. I showed Jeremy all my files and he told me he wasn't going to receive a credit on the film and his fees would also be separate from the budget already established – he was to be Bill's surrogate, his eyes and ears. I told him that I for one applauded anyone or anything that could get the film finished speedily.

Bill then spoke with our lawyers to assure us that the appointment of Jeremy in no way affected our credits, percentages or fees, which was much the same message I was receiving from Jeremy. With all this reassuring I became more nervous, but I never felt Jeremy was doing anything other than a purely professional job – and this was a film that could do with all the professionalism it could get.

After this meeting, I concluded my budget revisions and tried contacting Bill in California as he'd asked me to do. I tried and tried and tried – 17 times – without success, without one returned call. Eventually, I felt it was my obligation to send cables to both Bill and Rock Films' lawyers in London informing them of the new budget outlines and also requesting the further necessary funding.

I kept thinking I must be living in a black hole, since when I went to the viewing of the shoot at Ramport I was stopped by Sydney and Sandy Singh, the production accountant, before I could get to the door. They walked with me to Sydney's car. 'You're not to go in, Tony,' Sydney said.

'Why not?' I asked, more than usually fed up with this perpetual nonsense.

'Jeff's told Bill and Jeremy that you make him too upset when you're on the set or at rushes, and he's got the band to agree to your being barred from the set.'

I was once more perplexed and angry. 'But it was Bill who asked me to come back! I've been working on the picture for the last few weeks because he said he wanted me to.'

Sandy spoke in his carefully enunciated manner. 'Well, Bill doesn't want you there today, Tony. He told us both very clearly that you shouldn't appear.'

I thought about this new twist of fate and realised I had two equally unpalatable choices. I could force myself on to the group and create a scene, or I could walk away once and for all, completely disassociating myself from the manner in which the film was being concluded.

'OK,' I said to Sydney. 'You and I both know that the reason I'm not supposed to appear is because I can see through this crap and say so. That makes me unpopular but I can't carry on like this, so you pay me for the last few weeks I've worked and I'll piss off.'

Sydney and Sandy looked at one another in silent embarrassment.

'What is it?' I asked.

'Bill's told us not to pay you anything,' Sandy replied.

'Yeah, he's ordered us not to pay you a penny,' Sydney confirmed.

'And you're going to obey that, Sydney?' I asked. My tone was not friendly.

Sydney fiddled nervously with his ever-present briefcase. 'If we pay you, he'll take it out of our hides.'

'Do you think that's right? I've worked on the film because I was asked to and don't get paid. Has anyone else not got paid recently? Have either of you not been paid the last few weeks?'

'That's not really the question, Tony. We mustn't pay you because Bill's told us not to.'

I looked at them both hard and long.

Sydney opened his briefcase and extracted his company chequebook. 'We'll need an invoice,' he said, pausing with his pen poised above the cheque.

'Just give me my cheque and I'll get you an invoice.'

Sydney scribbled out his signature on the cheque, 'You know I'm running a terrible risk giving you this, Tony,' Sydney said, handing me the piece of paper.

'We feel very badly about this, Tony,' Sandy said, extending his hand to me, which I shook.

'Yes, we know this is madness but what can we do?' Sydney said. 'Keep in touch.'

Before I closed the car door, I reiterated my earlier warnings to Sydney. 'You should get off the fence. If there's gonna be a war, you've got to pick sides. Anyone in the middle's going to get squashed!'

This incident started a ludicrous, petty and nasty sequence of events that began with an investigatory audit of the film. As ever, I had been extremely careful in this regard, so I turned it around and made louder noises for my colleagues' itemised expense vouchers. Increasingly, I could see the tension take its toll on Sydney – he was aging in front of my eyes.

Another ludicrous situation arose when I was again asked to return and help prepare for another piece of the filming, but I knew that what was really wanted was for me to be the scapegoat again. When I asked if I'd be allowed on the set for the shoot I'd theoretically be arranging, I was firmly told I would not. I decided to keep my distance, and that was just as well, because just prior to the Cannes Film Festival Bill wrote a letter to Sydney in which he said he didn't want me to attend.

As for going to the Cannes Festival, I certainly didn't need to ask for Bill's assistance. I'd been going under my own steam since I was 17 – I'd even made a documentary about it called *The Festival Game* in 1969. I wouldn't beg a ride off Bill if I was in search of the Holy Grail and it was situated on the Croisette of Cannes.

In a strange way, it was a relief to see Bill's obvious dislike for me out in the open for all to see. I even enjoyed the knowledge that he was as aggravated as I was, albeit without justification in his case. I was fed up with everything and everyone involved on the film and my anger built with every new slight, real or imagined. Having been cut off from all but selected information, I can now see that I sometimes verged into paranoid territory, but I also know that more often I had good cause for my anxiety.

Immediately after Bill's letter to Sydney, I was dropped from the list of people to be copied in on all the internal correspondence on the film. I was not even named among those authorised to countersign orders. I only received copies because Sydney sent them to me surreptitiously.

On 15 May, the other shoe dropped – right on my head. I heard from friends on the film newspapers based at Cannes for the festival that advertisements for *The Kids* were ready for printing, but the names of Sydney Rose and Tony Klinger were absent. I was determined to stop this happening, and I didn't care what I had to do to achieve that end. I phoned my lawyer, Brian Eagles.

I then went to see Sydney, who sighed and nodded his head. 'Bill wants to crush me. They've got me committed to the Shepperton shoot and I still haven't got the money to pay for it. Right now, if he pulls the plug on me, I'd go up the spout for about £100,000. I'd like to just get the film finished without any more trouble, so we end up producing a worthwhile piece of entertainment. I'm in the middle of an impossible situation and have been since we started. I don't think I can win whichever way I turn, but I don't want to fight like you do – I just want to get this thing over as peacefully as I can.'

I'd never heard Sydney so low before. He'd been crushed before he'd even got into the fight. 'Sydney, you've lost your way,' I began. 'I don't want to fight. I never want to fight anyone if it can be honourably avoided but you can't box by the Marquis of Queensberry rules if the other guy's kicking you in the balls. If we don't get them to back off on the credits right now, we've lost the whole war and there'll be no way we can recover.'

Reluctantly, Sydney agreed to our being tough in our resistance, with the advice of Brian. During the next few days, our action on the credit situation bore fruit and our names were restored on a strip at the foot of the advertisement. Unfortunately, irked by our strong reaction, the other side became even more hard-nosed in their dealings with us.

Sydney was now being pulverised by the circumstances he found himself in. Everything he did, or we had done in concert, was under the microscope, and his already truncated powers had been almost totally eliminated as Bill's office took the reins of authority ever more tightly to themselves. Bill now took to telling Sydney, 'I'm the producer of this picture now your pal's gone, so it's gonna be how I want it. Anyone who doesn't like it can piss off, and that includes you or Jeff Stein.'

Strangely, I now started to receive formal copies of all letters again, although I never found out why. Perhaps the management team were simply making sure that they didn't breach our original contracts and give me something to attack them with.

Around this time, I received a telephone call from Keith Moon. He was pretty incoherent after he'd seen most of the film – perhaps genuinely shocked after seeing himself on the screen after a decade and a half, without make-up or a set of drums to hide behind. But he was still capable of telling me that he'd run the clock over the sections of our film and his bit needed to be longer and a bit louder. We had a bit of a useless conversation because at the time this was just another thing I was getting the rap for which I had very little to do with.

The conversation drifted on to other subjects as Keith told me he was again thinking of taking up an offer to make a commercial for McDonalds, and he was still considering various ideas on whether to do this for them. I had heard of this concept long before, and knew it had been quietly dropped by the giant burger firm when they had thought through the compatibility of their family-friendly image with that of the combustible Keith. It was part of Keith to suddenly let you know that he was still a major rock'n'roll star, a player with huge wealth and clout, even if sometimes this was far from the truth at that moment.

During this conversation, I came to the conclusion that Keith really wanted to be talking to Jeff and had probably got my number from someone in The Who's organisation when he'd asked for the film bloke's number. I liked the fact that he hadn't simply hung up on me when he realised his error, and so we were both having this meaningless, rambling conversation trying to be polite to one another.

Although he was falling apart, Keith was still oddly able to convince you, as he convinced himself, that he was indestructible. So, when he went on to describe some mad film he was about to make, I still enjoyed the chat, even though I knew it was probably total rubbish.

It was a story I think he'd heard from another nutty super talent, Peter Sellers. It started with one of those big car ferries that cross between England and France. For some reason, I think ransom, it was hijacked in the middle of the busiest sea lanes on the planet, and one by one the bad guys were dumping the cars, with passengers, into the sea. Of course, the hero was going to rescue them via a daring plan involving helicopters and suchlike. In Keith's version, he was the hero, whereas in Peter's it was him dangling from the chopper on a rope.

I now decided to visit the Shepperton shoot without an invitation, as I thought being there during filming was both my right and duty as the picture's producer. I arrived on the set just as The Who were launching into their first take. The shoot was being conducted on 35mm film and there were a couple of hundred specially selected, bussed-in Who fans in enthusiastic attendance for any necessary reaction shots. Jeff and I saw each other instantly but we both pointedly turned away from the other after a barely perceptible nod of recognition. I turned straight into Bill Curbishley.

'I didn't expect to see you here,' he said, as we shook hands.

'I thought I should come, Bill,' I answered.

'As you see, we can manage without you. I've got to go now but stick around, enjoy it.' He finished with a grim smile on his lips that was certainly not reflected in his eyes. I didn't bother to try scoring any further debating points. I was convinced that eventually I'd get my turn.

As Bill walked away, Sydney came over. 'What did he say to you? Anything about me?'

'No, nothing about you,' I said over the rising decibels coming from the stage. 'He told me to enjoy the show he'd organised. He was quite friendly, for Bill. How's it going?'

Sydney looked around as if the answer would come from the organised chaos surrounding The Who being filmed. 'Oh, you know, just a bit worse than ever. At least I'm allowed on the set, which is an improvement I suppose.'

We stood together as the band thrashed to the end of the song. Moon looked worse; his energy was almost gone after one number. Daltrey was glaring at everyone as usual. Townshend's gimlet eyes took in everything that he didn't involve himself in. John simply took no notice of the swirling madness around him as he sucked on the straws from two opaque plastic bottles attached to his mike stand. I never did know for sure that booze was in those bottles but they seemed an integral part of John's stage persona.

Ironically, despite knowing the band members as people and the phoney nature of the mini-concert they were playing, I was still in awe of their power once they ceased being four individuals and became The Who. The sum was greater than the parts. John Lennon once said that every rock act he'd ever seen live on stage was less impressive than the mental image he'd got from listening to their records – he couldn't have seen The Who on a good night. Something about seeing that four-man line-up going full throttle was impossible to capture on a recording. The Who were best appreciated live; even The Rolling Stones couldn't come close.

I only spent a few hours on the set during the shooting that week, as it was made very clear by the cold atmosphere that I was present under sufferance. During this period, I had several more conversations with Sydney, and there was a flood of correspondence between us. Sydney was girding his loins for the battles to come and was piling up as much self-serving documentation and evidence as he could, as I'd been doing since the film's inception. I also heard from two more of our cutting-room staff that they were leaving due to their frustration and the very strained attitudes in their department.

19

Bombed In Barbados - Brainless In London

As July arrived, I had one happy thought: at least everyone else on the film had grown to dislike each other with the same intensity they'd previously reserved for me. While the editing dragged on like some gothic horror story without end, Sydney was still madly finalising his library-film contracts. He showed me the corrected advertisement from the Cannes Festival trade papers and just to add salt to his wounded ego his name was misspelled with an 'i' where the first 'y' should be. He also told me that another shoot was planned for the 18th and that there would be a screening of the first cut around the same time. As I was going on vacation to Barbados on the 15th, I would have no chance to attend either, which really pissed me off as I wanted to be at both. Once again, I'd intentionally not been told until late.

Again, I offered to meet Bill to sort out our mounting arguments but without success. He simply didn't return my calls, so the day before my vacation I met Sydney to discuss everything, including his company's zero funds. We met at the tearoom of a posh central London hotel. It was interesting to contrast the place's genteel atmosphere, the overly correct formality and precise neatness with the slovenly, madcap gutter fight we'd become embroiled in. Looking over the fine china, I'd have had to be blind not to notice that Sydney was grey with fatigue and anxiety. His whole being seemed to have shrunk and bent in just a few weeks.

'Why take their bullshit, Sydney?' I said. 'Cancel the bloody shoot if they haven't given you the money. What have you got to lose if you stand up for yourself?'

He looked up from the cup of lemon tea he was sipping. 'Tony, soon I'll have to cancel the filming because I'll be left with no money and no choice, but I think it's best that at least I can talk to them, otherwise I'll be in the leper colony with you. Bill feels you let him down when you went to the scriptwriting job on the other film.'

'Do you know what the hell he's talking about?'

'No,' he replied.

'Tomorrow it could be you. No – tomorrow it *will* be you. I've said a hundred times that the only way to deal with them is from a position of strength.'

For the first time since we'd met, Sydney smiled. 'Not everyone wants to fight, Tony. I just want to finish the film quietly and get on to something new. I don't like this any more than you do but I've got a job to do and I'm going to see it through.'

I couldn't understand his remarkable restraint, let alone

agree with it, but as the only way I could attack them was via Sydney I had some sympathy for his thankless position of taking pot shots from both sides. We parted with Sydney wishing me a bon voyage and that he could come along. In retrospect, he might have been better off.

I left England for Barbados with my family and our friends, the Martin Birches. Martin is a record producer who's worked with Deep Purple, Whitesnake, Rainbow and many others of that type. It was a relief to arrive on that smashing Caribbean island away from the trench warfare. After a couple of days of too much sun, sea and booze, I had thoroughly unwound, as had Martin, who'd just completed his fourth or fifth album on the trot and was also in great need of rest and recreation.

One night, while our wives and kids were absent, we visited the bar a few too many times and sat by the pool in the moon's half-light, drinking our Pina Coladas and drunkenly swapping anecdotes about our work and some of the crazies we'd encountered. By about the tenth drink, I began to unfold The Who saga and Martin was in a suitably mellow listening mood. He was the first person not directly involved I'd told about it. It felt like I was getting a mental purge and, as we sat talking the hours away, I got rid of my bitterness in one torrent of words.

Martin, although he was as drunk as I was, gave me some salutary advice. 'You can't let them get to you like that, Tony. They'd laugh their heads off if they knew how upset they've got you.'

I thought about that for a moment.

'I suppose you're right, but I'm still upset even if I don't let on. It's just such a shame. It could have made an absolutely terrific film if they'd let me get on with it. I'm really angry because they took my dream and turned it into a nightmare. I can never forgive them for doing that. The whole bloody thing's become an endurance test. Life shouldn't be like that – there has to be some pleasure as well. It's a shame that dreams get chased away, that they become small, crumpled-up memories that you try not to remember so that they don't hurt you any more…'

The rest of our holiday was a notably good time, though without much more booze. We arrived home in mid-August to find 21 pages of letters from Sydney. The big event had been his sacking by Bill Curbishley, who had become angry with him because he'd told the executive element of the crew that money was running short again prior to a shoot at Twickenham, which Sydney said would have to be postponed unless he had the necessary finance. Mass panic followed this revelation, and Bill had then telephoned Sydney and said, 'You're fired!'

'Why?' asked Sydney.

'Because of your scaremongering and mixing it for me. You'd best get your next production ready, because the office you're in is gonna be closed!' Bill ended this speech by hanging up before Sydney could reply.

It was strange that Bill, who had no official function on the film, could dismiss Sydney. His action was to pose an interesting conundrum for the production, because, although Sydney had been sacked, his company was the entity through which almost every deal had been contracted. This led to a crisis meeting on 21 July. Present were Bill, Sydney, Jeff, Eddie and Jeremy Thomas. Apparently, it was a hot and heavy affair, since Sydney was said to have caused unnecessary worry to Jeff and Eddie when he'd told Eddie of the lack of money. Surely Sydney's very valid concerns for the production's continuation should have been the real priority. The lack of money was the root problem, and it had plagued the film intermittently from its inception.

The minutes of the next meeting were very interesting — and nasty. Sydney was attacked on every front and then discovered that all the final dubbing work was now to be undertaken in Los Angeles. Sydney later told me it was at this point he realised Jeff and Eddie had won every single one of the things they'd wanted. And Bill had told Sydney, 'I've got some bad findings for you and Klinger in the auditor's reports.' The whole affair was becoming ever more brainless.

20

Two Sides Of
The Moon

As I became increasingly immersed in two new films, I was losing my day-to-day contact with *The Kids*, which by autumn was at the Goldwyn Studios dubbing theatre in Los Angeles. I was also in California but my news of the film came via veteran staff members of the film who I'd originally hired.

One morning I woke up in my Beverly Hilton Hotel room and found I'd left my television on overnight, as it was quietly replaying the early news. Suddenly I was wide awake as I saw a picture of Keith Moon flash on the screen with the dates of his life and death at the bottom of the screen. I'd long expected it and it was bound to happen sooner rather than later, but it was still a shock. I telephoned Sydney to verify the report, since it emanated from London and it seemed likely he'd have more up-to-date information. He told me the English news reports hinted at a fatal combination of drugs

219

and drink, which had been too much for his abused body. Other than these rumours, the only certainty was that the Loon was dead; of that there was no doubt.

We talked about Keith and reminisced about him and his mad antics. As it happened, I was staying in the same hotel room he'd tried to invade with his pet tarantula, which he'd kept in a large glass jar. We'd only stopped that particular lunacy accidentally, by arriving unexpectedly while Keith was trying to creep into the lobby, glass jar in hand. I'm glad because I've never been partial to large hairy spiders, even if for some strange reason I liked that small hairy drummer.

Keith was only 31 when he died, but, having known him and his sheer zest for living, I figure he lived at least three normal lives in one and was about 180 when the clock stopped. He had a great sense of fun and mischief in his eyes, and he always struck me as someone who had a kind of mad genius for living life at super-speed, but who had unfortunately mislaid the off switch.

Of all the people I met during this nightmare, he was the one I grew to like. He was a man-child, never having lost the desire of a toddler to seek attention. But equally he had a razor-sharp wit and was at his most dangerously acid-tongued after a bottle or so of brandy and a couple of lines of coke at about four in the morning. Keith would assume the characters that he, in his playful way, thought we wanted to see. In one hour he could be Robert Newton, Count Dracula, Bob Dylan and Salvador Dali; and for him that was a pretty slow hour. His success destroyed him, but not without his knowing that was the price.

It's pretty obvious that a great deal of Keith's lunacy was born out of his insecurity. I don't know how it had begun, but I recognised it as one of the main drivers of his compulsive desire to show off. It was lost to many people that in 1970 Keith had been innocently involved in an awful car accident, which had led to the death of his driver, Neil Boland, a gentle Irishman with a young family of his own. Apparently, during a wild fracas with some skinheads, Neil had been pinned under the car and dragged along the road. As far as I know, Keith never passed a driving test, but I am going by two things here: one was that he told me he had never taken a test and the other was the way he drove, which was suicidal.

After the incident, Moon was breathalysed and found to be many times over the drink-drive limit and driving without any licence. This is when mayhem stops being any fun at all. Although the inquest cleared Keith, Neil's family never agreed and I think Moon never forgave himself for this tragedy. It did haunt him and caused some of his later, seemingly crazed actions.

Apart from the undoubted fact that Keith was, in his pomp, a truly great and innovative drummer, he was also potentially a bloody good actor. But again in self-defence, he totally overacted and this turned him into a cartoon cut-out Robert Newton. But during the filming and post-production I came to realise that Keith sometimes couldn't draw a line between reality and the role he was playing, either in our film or in day-to-day life. It had all become one for him, and, although the result was sometimes funny, it became difficult and later impossible.

221

Many others share the view that Keith would go to virtually any length to endear himself to anyone around at the moment, and win laughter or the reward of some applause. The truth was that Keith had legions of friends and followers who loved his boyishness and his whole shtick. Whenever you visited one of his homes, there were people hanging around, seemingly without any connection to Keith or to each other. Usually there was also a famous person or two, like a Ringo Starr or Rick Danko, but just as likely were some airline cabin crew, either trolley dollies or flight crew. You would find them lying around, recovering from too much drink and other things.

Keith needed chaos: he thrived on it. I remember being told to book into the Continental Hyatt Hotel when I visited Los Angeles by the band's management. When I arrived, they showed me to a suite that was clearly the worse for wear. Paint was peeling, a leg was coming off the settee, the furniture was stained and worn, and the television was on its last legs. When I went downstairs to complain, the duty manager said, 'You know the deal, Mr Klinger. When you're with The Who we give you a room that needs remodelling for a reasonable rate and you just go ahead and have your fun with it.' In other words I was expected to smash it up. Our nickname for the place was the Riot House.

One time Keith was walking through the lobby listening to the band's recording of its rehearsal. The manager walked up to him and asked him to turn the noise off. Keith politely did as he was asked and retired to his room. There he had quite a few detonator caps, which he'd been accumulating for the band's stage act. He then meticulously wired all these detonators to his room door and called down for the manager to come up and see him at once. As the man stepped out of the elevator he was just in time to see the door to Keith's suite blown clean off its hinges. Moon then stepped through the debris with the offending radio on his shoulder and said, 'That was noise, mate,' then pointing to the radio on his shoulder said, 'and this is The Who!'

Anything you wanted to do with Keith had to be coordinated with his assistant, gofer and right-hand man, Dougal Butler. Dougal was a lovely man who could make you laugh and who knew how to have a good time. He did keep Keith out of trouble, except when he forgot his job and joined in a bit. In fact, he and Keith were an explosive combination when the drink was in hand.

'We were on tour with The Who, in Detroit,' Dougal recalled of their lifestyle together. 'We were in this five-star hotel and we met the guy who played John Steed in *The Avengers*. So we go round to his room and we're happily having a few drinks with him and the drummer from Three Dog Night.

'But then Keith took a dislike to this guy out of Three Dog Night. The previous day we'd bought these gas guns, so we went and got them, got down on the floor outside the room, and let them off, bang, under the door. Then we hear all these dogs yapping. Keith goes, "I don't remember any dogs." We'd got the wrong room! It turned out there was this woman in town for some dog show. We'd gassed her dogs.'

Memorable as these larks were, as the 1970s gathered speed so did Moon's self-destructive tendencies. When The Who weren't working, there was a real fear that, if he wasn't given something to do, he might simply destroy himself. The solution? A solo album. 'The idea was, advance him some money and hopefully you'll get some of it back,' Dougal explained. 'We've got to keep him busy.' The virtue in the resulting recording – 1975's *Two Sides of the Moon*, a set of pop covers – is maybe more in its expediency than its music. 'It's the most expensive karaoke album ever made,' said Dougal, 'but it's a good insight into what he was going through. It's a laugh.'

But as Keith's alcoholism, cocaine use and susceptibility to the flattery of hangers-on grew under the Californian sun, the laughs steadily declined. Dealing with a drunk and drug-addled big baby with lots of cash can be a real pain in the bum, and ultimately, after a big barney and subsequent punch-up, Dougal took his final leave of Moon to work for Jeff on the film. Dougal was always most helpful as long as what you wanted to do wasn't against Keith's best interests.

It was a meeting with Keith's famous neighbour that made him realise he had taken the right decision. 'Steve McQueen came out and shook my hand,' Dougal told us. 'He said, "I love Keith. But you've got to move on – you can't live like that."'

I later discovered that Keith was furious with everyone, including me, for 'stealing' his assistant to work on the film. It had been Jeff who had approached Dougal but Keith lumped us all together and left messages for Dougal in which he wrote, 'You're licking producers' arses. Good luck, Moonie.'

I thought it was just a funny piece of nonsense from Keith, but I later found out it really mattered a lot to him — and Dougal. Keith didn't have many true friends and Dougal was his only real mate. Their relationship was very important to Keith, while Dougal saw himself more as a friend than as a paid employee. Our film had screwed up this relationship and, in doing so, probably removed one of the last safety nets that Keith had. Dougal had been a little bit of sanity around him. With him gone, there was nothing left to protect him except Annette, and Keith never listened to her wise counsel, I think simply because she was a woman.

Despite everything, Keith was amazing, and I am very privileged to have crossed his path as it zigged and zagged through life. Keith, wherever you are, I'm sure it can't be boring with you there.

21

The Last
Chapter

After Keith's death, I asked Sydney if he knew where the funeral was taking place because I wanted to send a wreath. Subsequently, I sent a condolence telegram to the group but Sydney wasn't permitted to know where or when the funeral was taking place. Consequently, neither of us was present and we weren't even able to send a floral tribute. What harm our wreaths could have done I didn't understand, but at least Keith and his celestial wrecking crew know some people did care about him.

A subtle change now entered the atmosphere of the film. Conciliatory feelers were put out to me by some of the people who'd been steering clear of me previously. The accountants even asked me to peruse the film's accounts, which were growing ever more alarming. The American sound-mix costs were astronomical, through no fault of the studios, and were much higher than I'd thought possible in my very worst nightmares.

In October, I met Bill and his wife Jackie for lunch next door to my office in Clifford Street, Mayfair. It was the first time we'd seen each other in months and, although Bill and I were initially wary of each other after all the bad blood between us, we managed polite civility prior to discussion of the film itself. Bill told me that the band were totally fed up and didn't want to spend another dollar on the film but had to in order to finish it. Although it was too late to benefit the film or me, at least I was being partly vindicated. It's good to be proven right even if I was one member of a very exclusive club that knew it.

Much to my surprise, we were able to cobble together a peace agreement within an hour. It transpired that Bill now didn't feel I was such a bad boy after all. Taking up the olive branch, I agreed that litigation only had one set of winners, the lawyers. We almost got chummy; it must have been the wine. Our agreement was to kill all our problems in one go. There would be no script credit on the film for anyone, which I thought fair since no one had eventually written a script as such. I would share my producer's credit with Bill, with my name coming first. I was to be invited to a private screening immediately and would be formally invited to all screenings including press, trade, magazine and premieres.

The next point was that we agreed not to badmouth each other in any way. I genuinely don't believe stating the facts in this book could be construed as badmouthing, which I feel means saying something truly nasty about someone, without any basis in fact. Next we agreed not to take any legal action against each other for anything that had happened previously.

I was agreeably surprised by the amicable manner in which Bill made these proposals but disappointed by his total rejection of my idea that he should meet with Sydney to reach a similar deal with him. Naturally, I sent a memo of this meeting to my lawyer so that he could put this agreement into formal language. A pile of letters followed in which Bill repeatedly stated we did have a deal but his lawyers were simply not finalising things quickly enough. He also stated this to me on the telephone, but nine months later it still had not been signed by Rock Films. By this time I was so fed up with it that I gave up chasing around in circles, so, for reasons I'm not privy to, their side of our peace treaty was never signed.

At the time, however, no one knew that this would be the case and Sydney became steadily more upset that he'd taken my former position as the odd man out. What made matters worse was the accountants' new insistence that they wouldn't OK any expense vouchers unless I counter-signed them, which put me in the invidious position of having to check Sydney's accounts so that they wouldn't remain frozen. As part of my peace deal with Bill, I supposedly now had a direct deal with Rock Films, which meant Sydney had to sign another agreement with me voiding some of the terms of our original, now partially defunct contract.

In February, I heard from Bill and other sources that the film's finish was still delayed for reasons beyond our comprehension in Los Angeles. It was now more than a year behind schedule.

Eventually in April I was invited to see the film, and I walked into the dim Wardour Street screening room with very mixed emotions. Part of me wanted it to be a great film for purely selfish reasons. Similarly, conceit made me wish it bore some of my imprint, while another dark side of my character hoped it all fell flat on its face because of the way I'd been treated.

The room went dark and the film played…

22

Take A Bow

For those of you who haven't seen it, *The Kids Are Alright* starts with a clip of the band on American television in *The Smothers Brothers Show*. After introducing themselves to Tommy Smothers and America, they play 'My Generation' and, as the song ends, Pete smashes his guitar and Keith's drums explode. Smothers, the audience and the band all look and sound equally astonished. Keith had put far too much explosive into his bass drum.

The opening credits roll and we see the young, aggressive, Op-Art Who rock into a live rendition of 'Can't Explain' on an old *Shindig* TV show. The film cuts to idiosyncratic English talk-show host Russell Harty swapping banter with the band. 'The wonderful, The Who ... The decade of The Who,' he says.

'Decline of The Who' quips Keith.

'The Who decayed,' says Pete.

Suddenly they are up on the stage pounding out 'Teenage Wasteland': Keith looks as wasted as the tormented lyrics.

Then while Pete does a silly little dance they play a bluesy version of 'Shout and Shimmy'.

The film now cuts back to Russell Harty. 'Let's get ourselves together – apart from The Rolling Stones, you're the longest surviving group?'

Pete replies, 'Well, the amazing thing about The Who is how incredibly nasty we all were.'

'Were?' asks Harty.

'Well, still are actually,' Pete concedes, laughing.

More songs in different concert settings follow before Ringo Starr appears with Keith Moon, generally clowning for the cameras. Pete explains to Melvyn Bragg how the band had originally made £387 one week and spent £1,300, mainly because of the guitar destruction he was encouraged to undertake for the cameras or the newspapers. Pete added that if he needed a guitar he'd nip into the instrument shop and borrow one. What made things worse economically was that Keith liked to join Pete in his destructive happenings and would smash his drum kit to be part of the fun.

After watching Keith being whipped in the Pleasure Chest in California – which is bizarre and funny as he stands there in little more than a black leather mask, blaming the publicity people for creating his strange public image, which obviously was untrue – the film cuts to the director of *Tommy*, Ken Russell, on British television. 'People like The Who can save the UK,' he states emphatically. 'They've more chance than [Prime Minister Harold] Wilson or those crappy people can hope to achieve.'

That statement is followed by a strangely sweet, insipid

version of 'Tommy', with the band looking oddly ill at ease and self-conscious. As the last chord dies away, Ringo and Keith reappear. Ringo, now fairly well into his 'medicine', asks Keith, 'What about the little singer?'

Keith's eyes become saucer-like. 'He's not a bad little chap,' he replies. 'Defenceless apart from that little mike, which he twirls around and around to protect himself from the vegetables aimed at him by the audience – slices it all up, gives me a nice, desiccated, mixed salad.'

We next see 'Pinball Wizard' from an oversized outdoor concert and then cut quickly to a German TV interview of Pete and another song from Woodstock, 'See Me, Feel Me, Touch Me'. Townshend says, 'Thank you,' as the huge audience roar their approval. We cut to Townshend being interviewed in London.

Question: 'About Woodstock – what did it change?'

Pete doesn't pause to consider. 'It changed me, and I hated it.'

Again, we cut to a sequence of guitar smashing by Pete, which segues into a very early interview of Pete as an embryonic, self-conscious rock spokesman, 'A large part of the audience is thick … Resign yourself to the fact that it's basic Shepherds Bush [in West London where The Who began] enjoyment. You do something big on stage and a thousand geezers are gonna say "That's good" …'

There's now an early Op-Art period rendition of 'Anyhow, Anyway, Anywhere', which goes to prove that old rock'n'roll TV shows aren't as good as we remembered them.

Pete Townshend then explains in pretentious terms why he

smashes guitars, contradicting his earlier account. He goes on to say the group gets on terribly badly, the singer wants everyone happy or he thinks something's terribly wrong, the drummer's totally unusual and John Entwistle's not seemingly interested in anything. During this, we see some diverse clips, culminating in the Entwistle sequence when he machine-guns his gold records.

Once again, we cut to a very young Pete being interviewed in an uncomfortable confrontation with a youthful but staid audience. One of them asks, 'What about musical quality?'

Pete replies, 'Steer clear of quality and you'll be all right…'

There are more questions and answers but that one's so illuminating I leave it in isolation.

What follows are three quick tracks using early promotional films and a German television show — 'Pictures of Lily', 'Magic Bus' and 'Substitute'. The songs still sound good. There are then quick interviews of Keith in a tour bus reliving early hard times touring in America, and Pete replying to the stories about smashing guitars, hotel rooms, etc. 'It's all lies. Not a word of truth…' His smile tells us different. Then, in another interview, Pete launches into an ambiguous explanation of why the band originally toured in America: 'We went because we were a bunch of English kids and we wanted to be in America.' The film cuts back to a very young, very self-aware Pete on the tour bus in America: 'Pop music is crucial to today's art, and it's crucial it remains art.' Immediately we see this art demonstrated with a wonderfully silly and dated promotional film for 'Happy Jack'.

After this ends we are back with Pete sitting in front of the staid early 1960s audience. 'Don't you think girls come [to see your group] for a sexual thrill?' asks a young girl.

Pete hardly looks up, 'No, because we're really an ugly-looking bunch.'

The crowd laughs.

'It's all mechanical stuff: smashing guitars, clothes, not glamour like other groups.'

Then in another interview Pete explains how the mini-opera 'A Quick One' originated, which flows neatly into Keith Richard introducing The Who's excellent rendition of it on The Rolling Stones' *Rock'n'roll Circus* film.

The film now cuts to the group meeting in someone's living room. As Pete says they are turning into a circus act, Keith stands on his head and denies the allegation. Again, we cut to another early audience interview of Pete. 'Are you stoned while you're on stage?' a young girl asks, to which Pete replies, 'No – we're stoned all the time.'

Back at Malibu Ringo Starr asks Keith, 'How did you join The Who?'

'I've been sitting in for the last 15 years. They never actually told me I was in the group – I knew it by instinct.'

Pete then explains how The Who and Keith originally met, which leads us to the manic 'Magic Bus' promotional film.

Now Steve Martin introduces Keith as the World Champion Hotel Room Smasher Up for the great American television viewing public. Keith obliges with carnage and mayhem, smashing the room and Steve Martin. We cut back to the 'Magic Bus' film, then on to Keith as the lunatic fireman arriving at Shepperton. After he solos on the drums we cut to the long-suffering Russell Harty, who's still trying to make sense of his guests. 'What did you do before you were a group?' he asks.

John replies, 'I was in the Inland Revenue.'

Roger: 'I was a sheet metal worker.'

Keith: 'I was a rust repairer.'

Harty: 'And you, Pete?'

Keith interrupts – 'He was arty farty.' Keith rips Pete's sleeve off.

Then there are more frantic moments with Keith and Ringo before Pete launches into an explanation of his performance. 'I'm not in control of myself when I'm on stage. If you came on stage with a microphone I'd probably kill you. I nearly killed Abbie Hoffman when he walked on stage at Woodstock. At the Fillmore a policeman came on stage because the place was on fire and I kicked him in the balls… I have to be a different person to do my job.'

Immediately, we see the group at Woodstock playing an instrumental. Townshend says he can't carry on whirling his arms forever – he's beyond that. There are then several good quick cuts leading to the original Shepperton shoot, the first thing we'd filmed.

As this ends we see Roger Daltrey speaking to us, 'The next thing is to get back on the road. You couldn't pick four more horrible geezers that make the worst noise you've ever heard in your life.' Roger says this with such force and good humour you couldn't disagree.

Fittingly, the film now cuts to an awful reggae version of 'My Generation' shot at an open air concert at Charlton, London.

After this, Pete is again captured in another interview. 'We do the music loud so people have to listen.' This naturally segues to Shepperton and Pete explaining that he's going deaf, and the doctor suggests he learns to lip read.

The Russell Harty interview reappears as Harty asks, 'Have you earned enough now to stop tonight if you want?'

Pete replies, 'Well, I have 'cos I write the songs.'

The rest of the group humorously attack Pete for this statement.

Next we cut to Pete in an old interview being asked, 'In "My Generation" you wrote, "I hope I die before I get old." Do you mean that?' Pete replies quickly 'Yeah.'

Years on, another interviewer puts the same question to an older Pete, who this time pauses and says 'Eh?'

Now the film cuts to Pete on stage, this time for the Kilburn concert. 'I've got a guitar up here,' he says, glaring at the fans, 'unless any little big-mouthed fucking git wants to come up here and take it off me.'

No one responds. The group then plays brilliantly.

As the concert sounds die, we cut to Roger: 'Rock'n'roll's got no future – it don't matter.'

Cut to John, 'We became rich and famous a bit later than I expected; now I'm too old to enjoy my money.'

Then we're back with Keith in his Malibu home and the camera is looking down at him as he sits on a large settee, stroking his beard. From off screen Pete Nevard, the cameraman, says, 'Can you really tell us the truth now and stop lying?'

For once Keith stops kidding around. He shakes his head, clearly angry. 'No. The truth as you want to hear it – no, I can't do that. You couldn't afford me.'

We don't have a chance to grasp this reply before we're back with Pete in another question-and-answer session: 'You're a very different person now to the desperate young man of the early 1960s, aren't you?'

'Yeah,' Pete answers, 'I'm a desperate old fart now, but [he laughs quietly] not boring though!'

Then from Ramport comes the 'Who Are You' song, which is excellently filmed. (This is the shoot I was banned from.) When it ends, the movie cuts back to *The Russell Harty Show*: Pete and Keith are ripping each other's clothes off and the whole group is verbally abusing the bemused Harty.

Next we see a good old-fashioned psychedelic rendition of 'My Generation' with Keith and Pete smashing their equipment up as the song ends. Then John says, 'I can't think of anything to say,' before Roger says, 'Rock'n'roll has never stood up to dissecting at close range, so the best thing to do is shut up.'

Finally, Pete talks about disappointing the fans: 'It's not the show must go on, otherwise you'll let down the fans. It's you've gotta go on, man, or the kids will be finished. That's rock'n'roll.' He ends just as 'Won't Get Fooled Again' roars into our senses. This wonderful tribute to the power of The Who live on stage is a fitting finale to the film.

The end credits roll over various scenes of Who mayhem and carnage.

It was a strange experience for me. The picture was better than I'd feared but not as good as I hoped. Conceptually, it was faithful to Jeff's and my original writing and obviously I recognised all the material we'd fought so long and hard to obtain and shoot. The film reflected the band's erratic history but stood as a celluloid monument to Keith Moon, whose sheer zest for life burst from the screen.

Unfortunately, although the picture had obviously been lovingly and professionally polished, it had one major flaw: it was too much the subjective work of a fan. Jeff's hero worship of Pete and the band dominated to the detriment of the average prospective viewer, who would demand more value for his cinema ticket. As a Who movie, it was an excellent achievement. As a rock movie, it was one of the best of a very poor field. As a film, it was good but not great. Still, there were a few priceless quotes from The Who and others, which I was glad to see had survived the editorial process.

At the end, I felt a twinge of stupid, dumb envy at the size and prominence of Sydney Rose's credit, but almost instantly realised he had more than paid for that prize. Seeing my name being linked to Bill's, both as producers, almost made me angry again, but then I remembered I didn't wish to pay any more for my prize.

When the lights came up I found myself facing Bill. We agreed the film should be cut by about 10 to 15 minutes because it contained a couple of extraneous sequences which slowed its pace, but I thought of the classic film adage: if a scene drags, reshoot it or eliminate it. Cutting a slow scene down only shortens it — it's still slow, but now it's just a bit shorter.

I told Sydney that I didn't think we were going to see any profits from the film, which unfortunately wasn't as commercial as we believed it could have been and had cost more than it might have. I was also concerned that, without Keith, the band wasn't going to be in a position to promote the film in America, which was the only possible way I could envisage that might give it a big send-off in the public's mind.

The film finally opened three months later. The critics were generally more than kind, and I quote the 20 July *Hollywood Reporter* review by Robert Osborne as an example.

> Wanna see (and hear) a scrapbook on The Who?
> That's what *The Kids Are Alright* essentially offers,
> and it's gangbusters. The New World release of the
> Sidney Box Production should get hefty support
> from rock devotees, and it even delivers a good
> time to anyone who might wander into the theatre
> by mistake.
> The film, directed by Jeff Stein and edited by Ed

Rothkowitz, is essentially a feature-length montage of past-and-present glimpses at The Who quartet (Roger Daltrey, Keith Moon, Peter Townshend, John Entwistle) during concert and TV gigs and off-beat interviews. It helps that The Who, collectively and individually, is unpredictable and colourful, and also that Stein and Rothkowitz are masters at tracking them.

Any documentary-style movie either succeeds or falls depending on the concept, and the approach here is a good one. It presents the various faces and growing impact of the rock group by zipping back and forth in time, *sans* any narration, without tackling extracurricular territory such as private lives or the backstage rock world. The film doesn't die, but still socks across its impact by showing the inroads of time on The Who's music, and their faces. The result is a fascinating, breezy equivalent to an indoor roller-coaster ride.

Picture opens with an introduction to the lads by Tommy Smothers on a 1964 TV show, then retrogresses quickly to a Who turn on *Shindig* circa 1966. Then ahead to the 1970s, and so on. Ringo Starr and Steve Martin are among the familiar faces included and, despite short footage on both, offer extra publicity value for selling the film.

Music, of course, abounds. Some 26 Who songs get either full or partial treatment, beginning with their breakthrough 'My Generation' and including

'Pinball Wizard' (done at Woodstock) and
'Tommy', which brought them initial motion
picture prominence in 1975. Snappy interviews
also spice the proceedings, as when Daltrey admits,
'We make the worst noise in the world,' and
Townshend deadpans, 'We're pop art, not quality; if
you steer clear of quality, you're all right.' Moon is
consistently outrageous; he's also poignant
inadvertently, since his drug-related death last year
shortly after completion of new concert scenes for
the film.

Some of the footage is in black and white, much
of it excellently blown up to 35mm from
videotape. Stereo sound recording (and re-
recording) is superb, and creates the proper assault
on the eardrums, while camerawork by a team of
experts does the same in the visual arena. Everyone
involved, in fact, deserves a bow.

OK, we'll take one, but now you know why I'll be looking
over my shoulder as I do so. And poor old Sydney didn't
even get his name correctly included in this rave review. His
name isn't Sidney, it's Sydney, and it isn't Box, it's Rose. I
hope the little big man rests in peace, alongside John and
Keith. Strange bedfellows indeed.

23

After The Ending

Harder, tougher, faster – these seem to be the words we all had to live our lives by. And what did that achieve? Not a great deal. We might have looked stupid in our funny clothes, with our puffed-up self-importance and over-grand eloquence, but we were all a bunch of kids, largely having fun, and not knowing any more answers then than we know now. The difference is that now we know that we don't know.

The Kids Are Alright did moderately well overall – quite well in the big industrial cities, but very soft in the southern states of America and predominantly black neighbourhoods of England. The distributors felt that the results were as good as could be expected without heavy promotion by the band. But I never received a full report of the film's income from anyone or a penny, despite my contract. The album of the film did sell very well in the US, according to the sales figures released to me by a friendly source within MCA – who also told me that they'd never been in doubt that there was going to be an album.

Time has not been kind to some of the participants. Several of them have died and, although it's inevitable that we will all die, it's very sad when it happens before your time. Where do gods go when they are finished, when they're found to have feet of clay like the rest of us?

I never met the group as a unit again, which I imagine doesn't disturb them at all. Roger expressed an interest in starring in a screenplay that I wrote but it didn't happen. He has matured into a much more rounded man. Now substantially self-educated and well read, he has added to his singular edginess with dignity, grace, love and generosity.

Pete Townshend announced that The Who had produced *The Kids Are Alright* themselves, something that could only be claimed if you call being the financiers producing. This only demonstrated how little Pete understood about the film-making process and all the work I and everyone else on the production team had done.

I don't know the truth or otherwise of some of the stories about Pete and I'd prefer not to go there because I have no direct knowledge about such matters. All I can say, for sure, is that I never witnessed anything in Pete's character that would lead me to suspect for one moment that he was a danger to anyone else and nothing has happened to change my mind.

Townshend is a giant as a player, stylist and composer, but Wagner was a composer of genius and he had one or two bad character traits. Van Gogh was one of the greatest artists of all time and he cut his own ear off, so Pete's behaviour seems mild in comparison.

I can't pretend to any liking for John, who was dry and very dark; even his sense of humour had cobwebs hanging off it. But I hope his demons were put to rest before his death. Always the quiet man, he turned out to have been leading a pretty hectic life in the hinterlands of his middle years; it finally caught up with him when the nasty substances eroded the last bastions of his failing, well-used body. He was an adult, it was his choice, and he was never the brightest person, but my guess is that he had a smile on his face when he went.

What can I add about Keith? He was like a demented general leading the ranks of the wild men of rock'n'roll; as such it only seems fitting that he died with his boots on. I enjoyed almost every minute of my time in his company — even when it got scary and out of control, it was funny and exciting. But being in his orbit for a while exhausted anyone near to him. Keith just wanted to shake everyone like a big kid, to get their attention, to make them really alive, and the way he chose to do this killed him. He never changed, never slowed up and never compromised his lifestyle. How much can anyone drink or do drugs? How many balconies can you jump from? How many explosions, car wrecks and abuse can any human being survive? Inevitably the machine eventually shouted, TILT!

The mystery for some is how the original Who survived so long as a band. The fighting was famous, non-stop and real. That never meant that the four men who formed The

Who didn't get along, because they did. They were like any other four men who worked together and sometimes argued about the best way to proceed. Mostly they discussed everything like civilised human beings, and only when they couldn't resolve things amicably, then they might hit each other.

The Who were never great mates socially, but they were, and to some extent remain, a musical and social phenomenon. Never seeking perfection, led by the conscience of Townshend and latterly Daltrey, they aimed, somewhat erratically, at being social idealists. Townshend states that rock music doesn't change the world but good rock music can reflect society, good and bad. Whereas Daltrey says rock music is the one thing that governments can't control, however hard they try, and even in places with barbaric regimes rock music will surface and will be the voice of the young. Music can affect people but the audience don't want to be lectured.

Anger is the blanket that surrounds Townshend, but it blunts and blurs his sense of proportion. Pete sometimes seems more confused as a human being in his early sixties than he ever was when he was a kid. How many times has he said, 'This is definitely the last Who reunion,' and then done the opposite? I would understand it if he only did those 1990s Who reunions for the cash – who could turn down such sums of money? – but I don't believe that was the motivation. Despite Pete seeming pretty much at peace with himself, every now and then he tries to recapture some of the old days' glory, sometimes successfully, sometimes not.

But I am convinced that Townshend and Daltrey work together artistically better now than since the beginning of the band, and also, as people, appreciate each other. As Pete says, they've now found a friendship that maybe they never had before. They can now talk openly about how much they love each other and that's wonderful.

As for the other main players in making the film, Sydney Rose eventually did make a deal similar to my de facto truce, but it only came into effect way after the events described. In April 2008, I received the sad news of his passing away. I don't know much about his later years, but I hope and trust they were kind to him; he was a well-meaning, nice and generous man.

As for myself, over my lifetime of creation and production I have learned to accept criticism whether it's deserved or not. I would rather be attacked for what I did than for what I didn't do. I hope I have been heroic enough to tell the truth in a timely and fair manner; this story and these people deserve that much.

Always remember this is about the music and the film. Picture the guitar arm of Pete Townshend whirling down to play those power chords. Keith Moon is sucking on the oxygen of life as he hammers at his drum kit. Entwistle strums those metronomic base notes, and it's all tied together by the blond boy in front with the whipcord body and the great voice, using the microphone like a lasso and dragging the crowd into sharing their intensity. That's The Who, purveyors of power.

It's hard to believe that Daltrey is not keen on his almost

perfect rock voice. Townshend doesn't really rate his guitar playing and sees his every fault writ large. The Who is a classic example of the sum of the parts being greater than the individuals. Yes, later it became stadiums and giant recording contracts, and replacement musicians, but this is about when it was still, just about, for real, just at the end of one era and the beginning of another.

Now millions of people hear Who tracks as the theme songs to their favourite television shows without realising who the group is, but at least it keeps alive a legacy of incredibly exciting music. I'm lucky to have worked with this amazing band when they were still all here, when there were more than dying embers of their fire and when passion still burned brightly. Despite everything, I still believe *The Kids Are Alright* – it's the adults who are screwed up.

24

Who Are You

Some 30 years on, the characters in The Who and the other folk involved in the creation of rock'n'roll's first disaster movie seem like bizarre creations set against a Dali-like world of outrageous excess, dirty deeds and brilliant performance. As strange as it may seem, I am still a fan of The Who and their music.

In Keith Moon's last interview on American television, to discuss the *Who Are You* album that had just been released, Townshend revealed how closely The Who are linked to film when he disclosed that their original manager, Kit Lambert, was only ever interested in making films about music and the band were simply a tool for him to achieve this. Maybe I had something in common with Kit. My interest was filming The Who in action like a giant art project. They fascinated me, and sometimes when you work with genius you can, like a moth, get too close to the flame.

It's easy to forget that rock is a visceral, gut music, not a thing of the intellect. But as the composer matures, so does the way he sees the world. As he perceives the shades of grey that come to him with growing awareness, the composer's initial gut reaction gives way to a more incisive, thoughtful look at the world. That doesn't suggest that anger is dissipated in the writers of true rock's older generation, or has become any less genuine or meaningful. I agree with Pete that it isn't necessarily only young people who can communicate with other young people, but rock has for a long time been a musical language regarded as the preserve of the young.

Perhaps this goes to the root of my problems on the film, since I believe that the group, particularly Townshend, lumped me together with what they'd call breadheads, people whose only concern is money, whereas I failed to understand that they still saw themselves as young rockers who were somehow able to mentally disconnect themselves from the facts of their financial responsibility and involvement on our production.

There was one meeting at Ramport that for me highlighted The Who conundrum. The group were talking about a young act that had been using their studio to record in and how they'd ripped up the toilets, written on the walls and generally made a mess. The Who were absolutely furious and outraged at this behaviour. Evidently, they didn't recall it was they themselves who had more or less invented rock'n'roll as devastation, but now they were the despised establishment and this was their hard-won property being damaged. Oh, how the wheel had turned!

At this point it has to be said that the band has a separate character of its own. When all four of the original members of the band were together, the sum of the parts was much more than the individuals put together, and much more appealing, and it is this that we react to. There has never been, however, a band consciousness.

In any assessment of The Who Pete has to come first. He is the inspiration of the band creatively, the engine. He is one of the giant figures of the world rock scene and whatever now happens will be remembered for centuries to come, not for what he is, but for what he's composed. There were two things that struck me when I first met him, his nose was not as prominent as I had thought from pictures, so it wouldn't be so difficult to photograph him looking OK, and the other was that his eyes were very piercing. But he always seemed like a coiled spring. His often erratic behaviour meant to me that he was either influenced by drugs, past or present, or was naturally a bit edgy and unpredictable; perhaps a mixture of all three.

Some of the people who will remember and perhaps study Pete will do so because of the way his music summed up the social changes of his life and times. What attracted me to Pete's work was both this aspect of his lyrics mixed with powerful music that rocked our society. Unlike most other writers he is equally brilliant and adept with both music and lyrics. His influence is seminal on many other musicians and has become part of the framework of our consciousness.

Townshend is the embodiment of all that is best and worst in a rock personality. He is a composer of brilliance, an original thinker, a very good guitarist, and one of the best showmen on the rock world stage. But Pete has clearly been affected by his own demons, including well-documented problems with drugs. I come from the school of thought that believes prolonged use of drugs adversely affects the user for life, physically and emotionally. Pete found himself caught between his prosperity and years and the claim he made when he was first famous; he hoped he'd die before he got old. He is the paradox of rock'n'roll; he symbolises his generation.

Daltrey and Townshend's perpetual conflict is, I believe, at the centre of our story. Whereas Townshend is introvert, tall, angular and dark, Daltrey is explosively extrovert, blond, compact and gives the impression of being able to look after himself. They disagree about everything and from these disagreements comes the motivation of this band. I think there was a very long period when they weren't even friends.

Roger was all right about the film going forward but wasn't thrilled about anything that wasted his time or cost too much. That was a waste of hard-earned money. I understood and agreed with that. He wasn't too keen on Jeff Stein, Pete's main fan, being the director. I don't think this was because he didn't like Jeff, more that he didn't know if he had the chops to pull the job off. No one could know the answer to that question, including Jeff, because he simply didn't have the proven track record to settle the matter.

On first meeting John Entwistle, I wasn't quite certain whether he was introspective or stupid. As I got to know him, I found him extremely introverted and dominated by the other members of the band. But when I probed more deeply I discovered him to be the intellectual equal of his colleagues and perhaps gifted with more natural talent. One of the finest rock bassists ever, John managed to hold together the rhythm guitar of Townshend and the frenzy of Moon's drumming, and the way he carried the melody line on his bass out front was almost unique and revolutionary for its time. He was the musical anchor of the band, and his excellence was the backbone of their work.

And Keith? It has long been one of the great 'what ifs?' of the music industry had Keith accepted Jimmy Page's invitation to be the drummer for his group. Keith's reaction had been coloured by his fear that such a split from The Who would go down like a 'lead zeppelin' with Pete, hence the name Page chose for his group. I don't know what Led Zeppelin would have been like with Moon in its ranks, but I suspect that The Who could never have been as big or successful without Moon. In fact, at that stage I don't think The Who could have continued. Keith was the magic ingredient that made the rest of the band work in its own nutty but exciting way. For someone so utterly without personal discipline, he still chemically reacted with the others as the catalyst that made it all possible. Before he joined the band it wasn't The Who and after he was gone it is never going to be more than The Who lite.

A large part of The Who's original fun was generated by their hostility to everyone including each other, but it isn't a pleasant or rewarding experience to be too close to organised mayhem. I still can't judge how many of the problems were generated by the people around The Who and not the group themselves, but I'm attempting here to establish the umbilical link between the essence of the group's creation, its continued existence in all its contradictions, and the way this destructive urge made me and any other outsiders on the film certain and necessary targets of abuse and misuse.

In this case, what you see is what you get, and – I suppose this is a backhanded but deserved tribute to Jeff Stein's choice of material – if you see *The Kids Are Alright*, you witness the bad and good, creative and destructive – the true band.

Epilogue

The intervening years have been interesting for me. Eventually we moved back to England when our first daughter was reaching high-school age, as we were worried about bringing up our kids far from their extended family. Strangely, our middle daughter now lives in Los Angeles with her children. For myself I am content to write my plays, screenplays and books. I have never quite recovered my love for making films, although I do still produce or direct sometimes, most recently with *Full Circle* in 2008. But I have been heavily involved in film education ever since *The Kids*, and I hope I have passed on some lessons from the whole adventure to others.

Did I learn anything that I can pass on to a reader? Yes, work and live with people you love on subjects you're passionate about. If you can afford to be picky, don't work with people who have different values. If it's wrong to start with, it will get worse as you move along. But I don't regret a single thing. At least I get to say I made a film with one of the biggest and best bands the world has ever seen, and that's better than regretting a lost opportunity. And I got paid for it. How bad can that be? I've been a very lucky man.

It's the dawn of 2009 as I drive down the Pacific Coast Highway on my way to visit a friend who lives on Malibu. The sun is shining; the weather is fine, gently warming my bones. I turn on the FM radio and 'Who Are You' is playing. This book is meant to be. I catch my reflection in the car's mirror: time might have passed by but now I know who I am and wonder if the same is true for everyone else.

Tony Klinger, Malibu 2009